Silent Keepers

"Readers can always count on the works of Janice Gray Kolb to provide universal insights and wisdom, as well as heartening passages of inspiration to provide hope for the soul. In her current book, *Silent Keepers*, she does not disappoint her many readers who look to her for solace, comfort, and compassion."

—**Brad and Sherry Steiger**, co-authors of the Miracle series.

"Jan and I have shared a deep friendship for many years, and I will confirm that she has been blessed with the ability to communicate beyond the limits of our own time and dimension. If this sounds incredible, I would urge you to read her books. Jan writes of the joys and sorrows of her own life, her words flowing from her heart so full of sensitivity and love into poetry and prose that is meltingly beautiful. Through her books she strives to comfort those who are grieving, provide encouragement, increase awareness of the beauty of nature and appreciation of our human relationships as well as stimulate the reader's own creativity. In *Silent Keepers*, she writes of her father and dear little cat with love and appreciation, and honors them with her inspired words."

—**Connie Gilman**, dear friend and friend of animals

"*Silent Keepers* is a beautiful memoir to my grandfather, Ellis George Gray, written by my mother, Janice Gray Kolb—and also of her cat of sixteen years, Rochester. Ellis and Rochester keep silent vigil of the author's life and heart—both then and now. While the story stands alone as a sweet and fascinating tale of love—it also serves to bring back your own memories and inspire you to relive them through your heart and through your pen."

—**Laurel Elizabeth Kuhl**, daughter

"There was only ONE Ellis, and I'm grateful to be able to carry that name on. I know that my great-grandfather, Ellis George, was an engineer and a wonderful, committed father, grandfather, and Christian. He passed away thirteen years before I was born, so I never was able to meet him, but the knowledge that I am named after him is an honor, and gives me an extra measure of confidence to pursue my career as an engineer, like my father, grandfather, and great-grandfathers before me.

"I am thankful for the life that Ellis George lived, for the father that he was to my grandmother and the grandfather he was to my mother, who lived with him for a time while my grandfather Kolb was overseas in the Navy. The legacy my great-grandfather Ellis Gray left helps to give me a foundation for my life and for my future. I'm proud to be named after such an incredible man."

—**Robert Ellis Hudson**

"When my grandfather and namesake, Ellis George Gray, passed away in 1977, I was 15 years old. His passing was the first that I had encountered in my young life, and had a profound effect on me. I was very close with my grandfather and grandmother and had enjoyed so many happy and fun times with them. 'Pop-Pop' was an important person in my life and I will always have strong memories and impressions of him. This book leaves me with strong feelings about a good man who left a lifetime of impressions on his daughter Janice, and on me, his only grandson. I also learned some meaningful things about him during his life and also since his passing as my mother has opened herself to his presence.

"As a dog-owner, I have a deep respect for my mother's relationship with her cat Rochester, and the incredible relationship that they continue to have years after Chester's passing. My mother's relationship and experiences with Rochester prove to me that my faith is real and that God works in so many ways to reveal things to us in ways that many would think unbelievable or unconventional.

"*Silent Keepers* is a wonderful reading experience that intertwines two exceptional and yes, seemingly ordinary beings, one human and one animal. It reveals to us that in their quiet ways both during and after their physical lives, they have had a profound impact on someone who has been open to their presence and gifts. This is such a strong message to all of us who are grieving or looking for greater truth and meaning through the passing of loved ones in any form."

—**George Kolb**

† September 8, 2009

To Doris —
With love and prayers,
Jan

Silent Keepers

Ellis and Rochester—
then and forever

† JANICE GRAY KOLB

Janice Gray Kolb

Blue Dolphin Publishing

Published by Blue Dolphin Publishing, Inc.
P.O. Box 8, Nevada City, CA 95959
Orders: 1-800-643-0765
Web: www.bluedolphinpublishing.com

ISBN: 978-1-57733-227-5

Library of Congress Cataloging-in-Publication Data

Kolb, Janice E. M.
    Silent keepers : Ellis and Rochester : then and forever / Janice Gray Kolb.
        p. cm.
    ISBN 978-1-57733-227-5 (pbk. : alk. paper)
    1. Kolb, Janice E. M. 2. Meditations. 3. Grief. 4. Parent and child. I. Title.
    BF1997.K65S55 2009
    155.9'37—dc22

                                                        2009015588

Drawing of Rochester on cover by Tom Peterson.
Drawing of Ellis on cover by the author (his daughter).
Photos of Ellis by his wife (my Mother) and the author.
Photos of Rochester by the author.
Cover photo of purple Rhododendron memory plant for Rochester by the author.

The butterfly is a symbol of Resurrection Life that Ellis and Rochester are eternally experiencing. It is a yellow and black Eastern Tiger Swallowtail butterfly on a glorious purple rhododendron

A portion of any profits realized by sales of this book will be used to support various animal charities.

Printed in the United States of America

10   9   8   7   6   5   4   3   2   1

*Dedicated
to my
beloved feline
soulmate
Rochester*

and

*to my
beloved
husband and soulmate
Bob*

and

*to Rochester's and my
spiritual friend
Chris Comins
who is a blessing and strength
on this continuing Journey.*

My Daddy was my hero.
He listened to me.
He was always there for me
when I needed him.
But most of all he was fun.

—Bindi Irwin
8-year-old daughter of Steve Irwin
(naturalist, environmentalist, Crocodile Hunter)
said in the Eulogy she gave for her Daddy—
September 2006

The fingerprint of God is often a paw print.

—Susan McElroy

Contents

PERMISSION GRANTED

I asked my Dad —
Would you like me to write
A book
About you?
He seemed glad
And his eyes became bright.
I knew that look —
I knew what to do.

And so I've been writing
With no apprehension—
For he's been inviting
From another dimension
To pray and to think
And we're each on the brink —
Of two worlds connected
But he's resurrected —

And I here on earth
Now tell of his worth —
Of this Dad strong yet mild
And his love for his child.
He calls me to silence
In this our alliance
I listen and write
He gives sweet insight.

It all seems so right!
Thank you, Dad.

Jan
April 20, 2007

BEYOND COMPREHENSION

Others saw him as a little cat —
    O—He was so much more than that!
      He made the sun brighten —
        the moon glow —
          the stars shine —.
            He was mine!

Constantly revealing
    secrets of the universe —
      he brought healing,
        love, joy, teaching—,
          he was divine.
            He was mine!

I was willingly reaching
    to learn, explore, give more.
      He was the door
        to another place —
          a world we shared.

Just gazing at his face
    life was rearranged —
      I was changed.
        We dared
          to live in another dimension.

We belonged to each other
    in profound love.
      We were bound
        yet it set us free.
          Our eternal bond
            is beyond
              comprehension.

For Beloved Rochester   Jan
for June 23rd, 2002
16th Anniversary of his adoption

from *In Corridors of Eternal Time*
Rochester's Book

Acknowledgments

May the words of this book—and the meditation of our hearts
(the readers—and mine)—give glory to God
all glory to my Christ
and love and gratitude to Blessed Mother Mary
who always intercedes.

I wish to thank my
Guardian Angel
and my special Angels
who are ever present.

I wish to express my deepest appreciation to Paul M. Clemens, publisher of Blue Dolphin Publishing, for believing in this book and for his kindness and grief support and to all his capable staff who helped in so many ways. I especially thank Linda Maxwell, Diane Winslow, and Barb Brumbelow for their fine work and their friendship.

I wish to thank Rochester for his constant love, presence, devotion, inspiration, and teachings throughout our life together. Because of him this book was written.

I am deeply grateful to my husband Bob for his love and support, for believing in me, and for our life together in New Hampshire. I am grateful too for the time he gave in endless hours typing this manuscript.

✖

I wish to thank
St. Francis of Assisi
and
St. Martin dePorres
for their great love and protection of all God's creatures.

✖

With eternal affection and in loving memory,
I remember beloved ones
who entered Heaven

✖

Bonnie Jean
beloved dog companion
of my spiritual friend
Dan Deane
March 2, 2008
and
Jack Clark
precious spiritual friend
of many years
in New Hampshire
September 17,2008

✖

In loving memory of Mr. T and Timber—
who will never be forgotten.
Beloved dog companions of Tom and Sue Peterson,
Christmas Week 2008

✖

We wish to acknowledge the passing
of a dearly loved friend and animal companion
A member of the Drakely family—daughter Jessica
and son-in-law Michael, Maxine, Renee and Clayton—
but very dear to us as well.
Isabelle
entered Heaven January 19, 2009

A Word in Preparation

If we would try to analyze ourselves in an attempt to find out why we became who we are, our first area of investigation may well be our parents. In those all-important molding years of childhood, the fate of the individual who would become "you" rested largely in their hands. This certainly is only a part of the whole development package, because we know of many siblings who matured under the same parents and similar environmental stimuli who eventually became radically different personalities. The old question of what is more important, whether we are products of environment, including parental influence, or genetics still rages. But there is little doubt that those who provided warmth, comfort, love, and home have profound effects. Their influence is inescapable and binding throughout the life of an individual. That influence could be vast or meager, exerted in a strict or permissive manner, be smothering or liberal, or even be planting seeds of good or evil.

In this book we are privileged to read the thoughts of an individual whose recollections of her father were as close to what she would consider ideal as it is possible to get. This in no way suggests that her Dad was perfect. She fully realizes his shortcomings in many areas of his life, but for her, the strength and steadiness, the love and wisdom that he provided were exactly the factors that she needed in her life. Although there were times of extreme contention and emotional pain in many areas of her life, her Dad was always there providing, without preaching, scolding or even disciplining, the silent strength she needed and depended on so heavily.

This book then is more than an attempt to honor a man who never made headlines, or influenced a culture, or provided leadership in science, politics, religion, entertainment or philosophy. It honors a man who was quite ordinary, but who influenced through silent strength all he came in contact with, especially his daughter who honors his memory on the pages that follow. The familiar quote by William Shakespeare in Twelfth Night of *"Be not afraid of greatness: some men are born great, some achieve greatness and some have greatness thrust upon them."* could be addended with *"and some become truly great by being humble, steady, and just plain good."*

But in this book she honors another who was not even human. His influence on the author was profound despite being bereft of any of the instruments that are normally associated with the ability to influence and change lives. His simple tools consisted of devotion, constancy, warmth, and silence. He was always there providing comfort and companionship when life for the author seemed to lose its direction, and the evidence that *"the sky was falling"* seemed unassailable. Sometimes a quiet, familiar and loving presence is all it takes for a person to *"grab hold of himself"* and go forward to face whatever challenge is there. He became a *keeper* as did the author's Dad. In this case a *keeper* may be defined as someone who the writer wants to keep and stay close to no matter what happens. In this sense it does not imply that a *keeper* is a guardian or jailer. Even things that seem to be of a demanding urgency are allowed to drift away as their importance dulls and fades, but a *keeper* is absolutely never expendable. In the title of this book *Silent Keepers*, the silence is part of defining who these two individuals were. In the case of her Dad, he was always a very quiet man. Never boisterous or loud, and never known to raise his voice even when provoked. Then toward the end of his life he became completely silent when his larynx was removed to quell the advance of cancer.

Rochester, her beloved feline companion, was also quiet his entire life. In the sixteen years he spent in constant close contact to the author, he never uttered a sound other than a muted purring as he cuddled with her. The single exception to that was when, as a kitten, he fell out of an upper window, hanging on to the sill with only his anterior paws. On that one occasion he let out some substantial screeches that led to his immediate rescue.

Thus we have the title, and a remarkable book about two very ordinary individuals. But ordinary does not mean unimportant. On the contrary it becomes a term of endearment and strength and extreme importance. We are all diminished because they and individuals like them are no longer with us.

Robert A. Kolb Jr.

Introduction

STORIES

By telling our stories
     the good and the bad—
          the failures and glories,
               the joyous and sad—
We touch other souls—
     that are listening to hear—
          a word of His knowledge—
               phrases, healing and dear.
Speak out your stories
     keep them not to yourself—
          share life's experiences
               they are health and true wealth.
                           Jan
                      May 30, 2001

Before the advent of writing, men would pass down stories and songs by word of mouth. Man's story became "his-story." and combining those words we have the stories of man becoming the "history of man." I would like to share with you stories and poems about two beloved males in my life, my Father Elllis and my cat Rochester.

Often the ordinary is where we find the sacred and in the simple act of story telling we may unexpectedly find God where we would least expect. Each story affects each person in a different way. We can never know a story's full impact on each individual. I have had tears when it seemed totally out of place to cry, and yet in hearing something spoken or reading something written there suddenly was a word or sentence or event meant just for me that touched my soul. It may not have been a spiritual account, but it held a truth within it for me, a gem that was mine. By revealing our hearts in relation to God and those we love, we truly affect others for good. Our stories matter! It is important too to tell little ones their own story. Telling them over and over they come to know in the tellings of the story who they are. They learn about their family as well. This did not happen in my own life as a child and teenager therefore much has been lost to me. You cannot always depend on memory, for in sadness or trauma life's passage and events are often forgotten or blotted out and sometimes do not return at all or only in part.

In a previous book of mine *Beside the Still Waters* I have written a meditation in regard to our stories and story telling. What I have written in there has become so much more important since then for after the writing of it I lost someone in 2002 I deeply love and whose Memorial Page is in the back of that particular book, and in a book that was about to be published, and too, in a Trilogy and book of poetry written after his passing in the years that followed. It will also be in the back of this book. And when I write "I lost someone in 2002" I mean only that his physical presence is not with me in the same way as before but his spiritual presence is ever present to me.

When I received my first inkling and touch of inspiration that I was to write a book about my Dad, I felt I simply had not heard correctly. I love my Dad dearly and was excited to receive a spiritual prod to do such a thing. But when I began to reflect on what I could possibly write to fill a book, I dismissed the idea. I thought I had written everything significant that I personally knew about my Dad and these various meditations are scattered here and there in my previous books. Those stories together would only create a fraction of a book! But the idea persisted when I prayed and throughout the days, and too, I was so restless and out of sorts because I was not writing except in my journals for I had recently completed my previous book *Cherishing.* Suddenly too I realized I was to write about Rochester in a different sort of way than I had been writing about him all these years since he entered my life, and remained in spirit after his passing. How could I write about both Dad and Rochester in one book when they had never met on this earth and were on the earth at different periods? Yet it was my Dad I had called on in prayer when Rochester passed away asking Dad to take care of him until I too one day joined them both. I knew my Dad would love that assignment for he also had deeply loved a sweet cat that will be spoken of in these pages.

And so, it seemed I had received my heavenly orders and I gingerly proceeded to write about my Dad. It was like searching the vast beyond because I remembered so little, not because he was not a precious Dad, but because of daily events in my growing up years that I have written about briefly previously and in a book under a pseudonym. These happenings caused a blocking out of some areas of life that I did not realize until writing the book just mentioned.

However—I learned anew and very dramatically something I have mentioned from time to time in other writings, and that is that if we keep our pens or pencils moving and just spontaneously write and not let ourselves stop for extended periods we are rewarded with some unusual memories, knowledge, thoughts buried deeply that surface, and other amazing things. And that is how this book was written along with adding the few stories I had written previously. I could not believe all the memories that came forth because I kept writing! Granted it is very little compared to some books on similar subjects, but I believe I have captured all that I was given. Some things may seem insignificant to a reader but when it may have been a past event I did not remember in years, it is a mini celebration to retrieve it from my past. I think my Dad was helping me write this, and I think he is enjoying it. You would have enjoyed him in life. He was and is a dear Dad.

And though I had no idea how I was to connect Dad and Rochester and have their heart stories overlap and interlock, that also happened in lovely ways when I kept writing.

Too—when I obey a leading—like beginning the writing of this book when I felt I could only fill a few pages, the angels seem to truly help when I step out in faith. It has happened to me again and again in other areas of life. And so as I timidly began to write this book in the Fall of 2006 two significant signs came to me, one in November and one in December, showing me that I had indeed understood this assignment correctly. To me they were rather overwhelming. I was still in awe of receiving the first (and still am as I write this) when the second one arrived!

The first came from my son-in-law Rob Hudson who out of the blue sent numerous pages of Gray family records to me by e-mail with no prior conversation between us on this subject for a good number of years. He often expressed concern I knew nothing about my background but we had not been in touch for such specific discussions for quite awhile, except for general family contacts, yet always knew the other was there. Rob had helped me personally in long talks concerning family matters many times over the years. It is meaningful to me too that Rob and our daughter June and family now live in our former home in Jenkintown, Pennsylvania where June grew up. Rob too had been interested in learning more about his own family background in the years prior to this and his own Dad had just passed away earlier that same year in February 2006. But the span of time about anything at all, discussed or otherwise, on this subject matter was sufficiently large enough to think this information he suddenly sent with no request for it from myself was unusual, most especially in its timing.

I was so thrilled with it despite the fact it was difficult at first to understand. Bob, my husband, was seriously checking it out also. Even if I could not immediately decipher it all, but which we have surely done since, it was an enormous "sign" for me that I was to continue the writing about my Dad. If that were not enough, only several weeks later for Christmas among many other things from her, I received a book from June that I simply could not believe existed. The title is *The Craggy Hole in my Heart and The Cat Who Fixed It* by Geneen Roth. The book is about the author's great love for her Dad and her beloved cat. I will say no more so I will not take anything of the story itself but let you find it for yourself to read. It is priceless to me and has not grown less powerful in its story after four readings. There will be other readings too. The author reminds me of myself in many ways in regard to her obsessiveness and great love for her Dad and cat—two who never met just as my Dad and Rochester never met on earth. Neither Rob or June had any idea of the book I had begun to write because I never tell anyone what I am writing until the book is completed and accepted. Bob is the only one who knows for he types all that I write in longhand. These gifts of family history and the book were truly blessed "signs."

Too, I had been reading a book about a famous father by his daughter prior to this, also multiple times as I do most, and I suddenly became aware that also was a "sign" to me to write this very book. I just had not previously realized it. I have quoted from it here and there in this book. There are very few books in stores concerning the loss of a beloved animal and grieving for your animal loved one. I have repeatedly in previous books mentioned *Maya's First Rose* by Martin Scot Kosins that I had read multiple times even before Rochester passed and continued to read afterwards. It had become my companion in grief, and Martin writes of his great love for Maya his beloved dog and the anguish of her passing. But I was reading other books as well multiple times. Grief is grief—be it for animal or human, and so books concerning grief over human loss helped me greatly too. In fact most books on grief were regarding humans and not animals that I bought and consumed. Anything I have quoted in this book by others who are spiritual friends to me now through their books and writings is because they so amazingly wrote feelings I have written in my own journals or thought about and wept over, or wrote in my previous books. Heart thoughts that only some can deeply relate to. I pray you can relate to this book as you read.

And so I wrote and wrote and the book grew and precious details surfaced about my Dad the more I wrote. I believe I have included all I know about him with only a few exceptions and there were reasons for these. I did not want to write about my Mother for I have done so many times, and so in order to not get into more about family life and to keep the writing centered on Dad, I had to leave some things from the pages. But of course there are some writings about my Mother for she was part of our life together. There were some difficult situations in our lives that I prefer not to put into Dad's and Rochester's book for this book is their book. Those incidents were not what Dad and Rochester were about. Dad and Rochester both symbolize great love to me.

As I was writing this book it seemed suddenly others were writing books about their fathers, all men doing this and not women. These were well known people writing, not someone like myself, but their Dads were loving average men. I saw several authors interviewed on TV.

As to the words in the title *Silent Keepers,* they have significance in regard to Rochester's and my Dad's precious spiritual care for me both while they walked this earth and now from Heaven. Both Dad and Rochester were silent. Rochester was silent all his life, and Dad the last seven months of his life. But Dad was always a very quiet man even when he spoke. And the words *"Silent Keepers"* have two meanings for me. Rochester and Dad were both *silent* and both are my very special heavenly *keepers* linked and entwined with God, Jesus, Mary and the Angels. Out daughter Jessica has used the word *"keeper"* for years in regard to someone or something that is out of the ordinary, precious or priceless saying *"That's a keeper"* or *"He's a keeper."* So to borrow her unique word I will most emphatically tell you as she would that my Dad is a *"keeper"*—and my beloved Rochester is a *"keeper"* too, most especially to me. Both are endearing *"Silent Keepers."*

When I was a young girl my little friends and I had a special place to gather during the war years of our childhood. It was on the large gray air raid box. These boxes were placed in strategic places in all neighborhoods and in ours it was on the side of the end house on our block of row homes in Philadelphia. I have written of this in the same chapter in my book *Beside the Still Waters* that I mentioned previously here. On summer days, or after school, or in early evening of gentle nights a number of us would gather on this wooden air raid box. It held about four of us young girls side by side, our backs against the stone wall of the home and our legs stretched down its slightly slanted gray top. It was on this box we shared secrets, fears and stories. It was a time when the stories shared seemed extremely important.

In the box was stored essential equipment to be used by designated air raid wardens in time of an air raid, either for a practice drill for one or for a real air raid that we fearfully prayed would never come. When the sirens would blare at night and our parents had to obey by pulling down all the shades so that no light could be seen in the windows, it was a frightening thing and my Dad was always a great comfort to me at those times. It was preferred that all house lights were turned off and this made it even more terrible. Search lights would often be seen flashing across the night skies while we were in the process of obeying the orders of covering our windows. I knew these were used to detect enemy planes and it was terrifying.

But in the friendliness of daylight or lovely summer evenings these large gray air raid boxes were a meeting place for children of the war years, and our box was unique and personal because of the private times we shared sitting upon it. It was a comforting spot. There was nothing frightening happening while we sat there, but left on its own it was often opened in the dark to the wail of sirens and the mysterious items within it were removed and used, items we never saw because we were behind drawn curtains .I see now this large gray air-raid box was a *keeper* of friendships and hope that drew us together, and too, a *keeper* of the equipment to keep us safe.

During the quiet times of friendship upon this latched container of war defense articles it seemed we could *keep* the war away. It was then we unlocked our hearts and confided fears and secrets. And always my friends liked me to tell them stories that I made up in my own heart and mind. And I did. At that period in my life those stories seemed to flow without effort and they cheered my friends and myself. At times one of my friends told a story too. Often at home I would write a story down after spontaneously speaking it out for my little girl friends, and that in turn comforted me to have it in written form in a note book, to reread when I was alone or afraid. I was transported in spirit back to the air raid box with my little friends, and their laughter and enjoyment then became gifts to me in my solitude.

The stories you are about to read in this book are true stories and reflections and sharings from my heart.

It is said that in some deep part of our memory is filed away every story we have ever heard. This seems incredulous! We carry them with us, and every story we have ever lived. Sometimes they are stored away until we are able to face them or that we have the understanding or capacity to bring them forth. In a sense we are reading them for the first time. When they do come back to us they may be surprising in their meaning. Without our being aware, we have been storing fragments and pieces of something greater that emerges over time. Sometimes we find too we are still not quite ready for our stories, or at least some of them. Often too they bring healing though to situations in our present lives. It is all a mystery.

I ask you now to climb up on that gray air raid box with me while I tell you the beginning true stories in this book. I think you will feel like you are younger and enjoy hearing them from up there. After that you can get comfortable indoors in your special chair to read all the rest of the book. You will know when to climb down from the gray box and go indoors just as we always did in those war years.

I pray, though my Dad was no one special except to me, my Mother, Bob and family, and others in his life that I never knew, that you will still be touched by his life and Rochester's, and find yourself remembering too. We all have the good and the bad. May this book help you to remember the good. It does not matter that you do not know my Dad or little cat. Soon you will. And they bring a message for each heart—and perhaps each will be a different message, but all will contain love. God so often through time has used the "little ones" to bring forth His most significant messages.

Through my extensive reading and my own life experience and knowledge of others I know personally, I know that it is quite normal for parental death to have profound affects on ordinary people. In some it remains inward through the passing years rarely discussed especially if there had been grave problems. The various forms of reaction to a parent's death are highly individualized, however no adult should realistically expect a parent's death to leave them unaltered. Your life is altered forever when you lose someone you love. You do not "get over it" as some may try to tell you. The person you love is the "it." You are never as you were before.

Too, this can be said for those who deeply love an animal companion for their passing is no less life altering and overwhelming than a human's and often may even have far greater significance. Many men and women, past and present have attributed their inspiration, quality of life, and spirituality and much more to the companionship of an animal in their personal lives. These animals are large and small and deeply loved, and many of these humans prefer to be only with their animal companions in a solitary life style and live lives of precious existence because of this. These humans are not strange. They have discovered blessings beyond compare and unconditional love, and when their animal passes from this world to the next, their companion is mourned beyond anyone else's comprehension. It is a grief of the soul.

I wish I had the same impact on my children as my parents had and continue to have on me. Perhaps because our six children each have five other "best friends" in having sisters and a brother, a concept Bob and I encourage to this day, and I as an only child had only my parents, the impact of my parenthood perhaps is not as enduring and strong. I pray it is but I can only hope, and I believe it to be to at least several of our children. I pray too that we as parents live on in our six children as my parents live on in me despite the many problems in early growing up years. Their legacies on earth and from Heaven are precious relationships made fresh and new and stronger ever since.

In closing may I tell you that it is important for me at all times to have sacred space and an altar. I have written on this subject in two past books. For me, my beloved Rochester is symbolic of the Divine, an Angel in fur, and God-given breath of life bestowed on me at a time when I needed both an Angel and an enlivening prod to begin my life of writing. My Angel often laid upon my large desk that also held my altar that he inspired. He still lies there—beneath an icon of Christ.

His presence has always been a blessing on myself and my writing. A precious animal like Rochester with his love, warmth and affection, who loves to be near you and petted, is a Holy presence where God can meet you.

Aside from the altar on my desk I have one too on a wide wooden shelf at my kitchen window. In addition to these two altars I have had a prayer chair, a wooden adirondack chair upon a raised platform by our lake since we have lived here, and this too is sacred like an altar and where I pour myself out to God in grief and in many ways in past years. It is the place I could not wait to climb up into after my Dad's death in Pennsylvania and the long trip to New Hampshire that followed. I cried and cried as the lake breezes washed over me. Creating an altar and sacred space is most important for your solace, reflecting, grieving and prayers and gratefulness for your loved ones.

If your beloved one has gone to Heaven in the past or in the present, a journal will help you in your grief and is a form of communication. It will not take grief away but you will feel like you are loving your dear one in still yet another way by recording his life that you treasured with all your heart. Your own written words and thoughts have a unique way of ministering to you. They are often like spiritual food for your soul.

Write about your life together and as you write you will cry as I have done all through the writing of this book, and previous ones, but your writing will be for all your life and you will value your journal with great appreciation and love. Only you can do this for your dear companion and yourself. On some other spiritual plane it will help you tremendously and honor your dear one. When you begin to write you will understand what I am saying.

Please may I suggest that you obtain a journal that truly appeals to you and keep it with this book as you read. You may want to respond to the book in your journal pages or begin to write down all your memories and thoughts too. Journaling helps us go inward and aids us in our journey. We give life on the page and we give life also to part of ourselves when we write.

As I have written in each of my previous books in similar ways, I will state that I am writing from a Christian perspective, but anything suggested in this book to do spiritually can be done according to your own personal faith or way of living.

As you read this book, know a little creature of God is present. My little marmalade and white cat Rochester has been completely with me in the pages of my twelve previous books which he co-authored. He was not yet born or in my earthly life at the writing of the first. He has remained with me in spirit since his passing and through my writing of our last four books, and now this one you are about to read. This book and any other I have written only came into being because his *"Angel Being"* came into my life. His love and presence are inspiring me and we communicate deeply. His paw prints are on each page. His essence and spiritual presence are there. He has helped me through his entrance into Heaven to experience too, my Dad in new ways. He is my Angel!

Perhaps if you have never examined your beliefs before, as you begin this passage you may wish to do so during the reading of this book. I believe in God as I have stated in my previous books, and in Jesus and Mary, and that there are Angels with me always. I believe in love, and in the love shared with my husband and all my family members, and the love shared with special friends. I believe that God can speak to us in any way He so chooses and I anticipate it, and too, the expectation of Angels making themselves known. I believe in the precious love of my little cat Rochester and that, as in life, we continue to communicate this love and all else to each other. I believe in the Afterlife and that our loved ones there are but on the other side of a veil that is often lifted and crossed. And too, I believe in the sanctity of life for all God's creatures as well as for humans. I believe in all of nature as other ways God speaks to us and is present to us, for I have experienced Him in these ways. Perhaps you may wish to examine your beliefs also as you begin and travel this corridor, and record them in your journal.

The meditations in this book follow a specific order and in spirit were given to me in that way. They build upon each other. The book is a portion of my personal journey shared with my Dad and Rochester. Instead of jumping around randomly into chapters as some do when reading a book, I would recommend reading it from beginning to end in chronological order. Reading in this way you are more apt to receive significant insights meant just for you. And I believe there will be a greater benefit in reading in this way for those in grief.

To those grieving I extend my deepest sympathy. I believe you will understand those are not superficial words as you read, and that my heart is in them. I pray this book will bring comfort as I hope my previous ones do each in their own way. Only those who have shared a sacred relationship with an animal can truly know what we experience when they pass. It is not the same as with the loss of a dear human we deeply love. It is not something I have yet learned to explain.

Many think of themselves as skeptics, and do not believe that your beloved one lives in Heaven and yet in spirit also, is ever with you as you continue on your life's journey. Even when proof of this is presented to you again and again you may have difficulty accepting that your loved one, be they animal or human, remains with you until you are reunited in Heaven. If you can consider this possibility, then perhaps it is time to become a most comforted believer.

A book that I discovered and have read many, many times since Rochester's passing and that gives me such utter peace, also contains dozens of passages well underlined that are referred to again and again. The book is *Walking in the Garden of Souls* by George Anderson and I share these lines that from the first moment I read them in grief in 2002 they have sustained me and blessed me more deeply with each reading.

When we experience the loss of a loved one, part of the profound change that comes over us is our link to a world we have never experienced, much less thought about. But the link to our loved ones can never be broken, not even in physical death, and it connects us to a world we now feel and can be affected by.

Please step into another dimension with me now and meet Rochester if you have never previously met him in my other books. And let me introduce you to my Dad Ellis. As *A Pilgrim On Life's Road* may you always remember them both and this portion of your journey as you travel *In Corridors of Eternal Time.*

God Bless You!

Janice Gray Kolb
East Wakefield, New Hampshire

MEDITATION ONE

In Eternal Time

For you, these may even live in a parallel universe.

—Unknown

In this corridor of grief we lose part of ourselves in losing someone important to us. If we dearly love this individual be they human or animal, when someone dies we die too. Pain of grief never truly disappears. We accept the fact that grief, like continuous waves rolling in and out on the soft impressionable sands of our heart and mind, will always come and go, will always be present. Our loved one's foot prints are ever in that sand and do not get washed away, leaving their loving eternal mark and imprint of eternal love for us. Grief is ever inside us and will never completely go away. It cannot ever be vanquished or cured. We can be overcome and ambushed by an unannounced and unpredictable wave of emotions, sorrows, and flashbacks with great unexpected suddenness.

I write from a passing of thirty years ago of my Dad and a five year period in regard to Rochester. It is all still as if in the present. It is a blessing and how I ask to live from God.

I do not learn to live in this way deliberately until Rochester passes. The presence of loved ones continues in a way not truly explainable when life is lived in this way. It is as if we are on the brink of two worlds and that there is an expectancy and vitality all about us as we live in the moment and believe anything is truly possible for we have not closed a door between us.

Only a thin veil hangs between
The pathways where we are—

states the first two lines of a short poem by Julia A. Baker, and God keeps watch over "thee and me." But sometimes we are given the incredible blessing of having a beloved one break through the veil. Yes! Still yet another poem by Rumi tells us—*that the door is always round and open and people are going back and forth across the doors where the two worlds touch.*—That is how I live and I am so grateful. I forever expect subtle and sometimes not so subtle contacts, signs, visions, dreams and all the inventive and amazing ways loved ones attempt to tell us "*I am here.*"

The other evening on a news program we saw and heard a man we did not know but is an American and doing important work. I choose to share what I heard and insert it here in my already written meditation. He began talking immediately saying he believed our loved ones who have died are ever around us and we can speak with them. Heaven is close. Because his words spilled out so suddenly, apparently because he wanted to give credence to his spiritual beliefs so his statements would stand out over the rest of the interview, he strongly stated them first surprising even the interviewer, I believe. I felt the words he spoke confirmed all I write here. He was like an Angel that suddenly appeared saying an "amen" to my beliefs.

I believe time is different and of an unusual quality for someone who is grieving. Even if it is many years in the past a moment can be retrieved in an instant. We live in an altered state or dimension. It is because we love the person or animal so deeply and they still live and are alive to us. I believe, as I frequently write, grieving lives in an eternal present—in the present moment. This ignores or defies ordinary thinking or any means of keeping time such as seasons, clock or calendar. It tells us love is eternal in this passage of our spiritual life that we travel upon forevermore. We are travelling *In Corridors of Eternal Time.* It is not wise to use the word "recovery" for that indicates you can return to the way you existed before your loved one passed. No, you never can. You never can.

We can never go back to that life. That old life passes away forever with the individual that we are loving for all time and eternity. We are different now. And yes, even stronger once we rise up.

I have written so much about grieving in my Trilogy that can be referred to if you wish. I am writing now of the true essence of grief that ever remains, but also becomes an inner inspiration and gentle force of indescribable love and comfort in every moment. These are not just words. I am living this now on the brink of two worlds.

Our loved ones who were and are life itself to us and are in Heaven still live with and in us and through us. Each time we recall a memory we are giving them renewed existence. We share things in life with them, the simple things we once enjoyed together when they were physically here. Our loved one is within us and with us. Rochester's *Anima* is within me. In a spiritual sense though his life continues on, our loved one is born anew. The words of an old Methodist hymn reveal truths about Jesus but now also speak of each of our loved ones—saying,

> *And he walks with me*
> *And he talks with me*
> *And he tells me*
> *I am his own —*

That is life as I travel *"In Corridors of Eternal Time."*

We are all on a road which will eventually take us back to them, where they are waiting for us in the grace and beauty of the hereafter. We are never alone in our journey on the earth.

—George Anderson, *Walking in the Garden of Souls*

MEDITATION TWO

Fletcher Works

*I am thankful I was given dolls as a child by my parents and that
I loved them so, for as an only child they and my stuffed animals were
dear to me. Dolls truly were prayerful to me. I prayed for them and
told them Bible stories and taught them their own prayers.*

—Jan, from *Beside the Still Waters*

It is a very special day today. I am going to work with my Daddy. There is a big Christmas party for all the people who work at Fletcher Works and Mother and I are invited. But Mother is not going and I do not know why. My Daddy and I drive down to the city to the big plant where he spends his days. It is a tall large brick building that takes up a city block, or so it seems to me. He is very happy I am going with him.

Once inside the building we go to the floor on which he does his job for the war effort. Many men, women and children are there talking and smiling and Daddy begins to introduce me to many of them. I am shy and awkward and quiet but I am still having a wonderful time. There are delicious snacks displayed and colorful punch in many large glass bowls. Daddy sees to it I have a little empty plate and we go to a table and pick out treats together then stand aside together to enjoy them. It is a happy party I will always remember and Daddy seems very proud of me. People like Daddy, I can tell. Just listening to their conversations with him and watching their faces I believe they think Daddy is very nice. He is. He is the best Daddy anyone could have.

After a lovely long time at this party people are slowly beginning to say goodbye to each other. Before anyone leaves a man walks across the room toward Daddy and me and with a big smile he hands me a Christmas present. Imagine—a man I never saw before gives me a present! Daddy tells me I may open it right now for it is a little gift to always remind me of this day. I gently remove the bow and open the colorful paper and there before my eyes is my surprise! I thank the nice man very much. He smiles at me. In my hands is a sweet soft rag doll wearing a colorful pink, blue and white print dress and a big soft ruffled brim bonnet to match. She is cuddly and cute and has funny large blue eyes that look into mine and she seems surprised. A black thin embroidered line circles her blue eyes and she has black stitched eye brows. Her nose is a pink embroidered triangle and her lips are created in red. She is unusual and sweet and her face and body and arms and legs are all of a soft white cloth material. I like her so much and right away hug her to me. I am so happy to have her. Daddy and I leave the party and the big building while others too walk along near us to leave also. I thank Daddy for a day I will always remember at his office as we drive home together. I hug my new little doll to me as she sits on my lap on the ride home.

I do not remember everything from that wonderful day for many happenings about my younger life have been blotted from my memory. But I do know that little doll was and is precious to me for she symbolizes that lovely party my Dad took me to and how proud he was of me in his own quiet way. We had such a beautiful time together. I do not remember what I named my Dolly and that is so unusual I would not know that, for names are significant to me. To this day I name everything that is mine. Perhaps I will give her a name now after I pray about it all.

At some point in my life, I believe it was after both my parents had gone to Heaven, I rediscovered all my dolls there in their home. I divided them amongst my five daughters. For ten years three dolls sat on a bookshelf in the entrance hall of a lovely old Hitching Post Village Inn in Center Ossipee, New Hampshire that our daughter Jessica and son-in-law Michael proudly owned and ran as a Bed and Breakfast. It was so soothing to often walk by my dolls sitting on that shelf. One was a Shirley Temple doll. They were my little friends in the long ago.

But the little rag doll, my treasure from a magical day spent with my Dad in a big old factory in Philadelphia, is such a joy even though I cannot hold her. She is an *"Earth Angel"* to me. She belongs to our daughter Barbara in Jenkintown, Pennsylvania, and on Barbara's kitchen wall is a woven tan scoop-shaped basket with the front rim of it all around painted red, and a woven handle at the bottom. Sitting inside the scoop, like it is her little chair, my rag doll is displayed for all who come into Barbara's kitchen. My doll really is unique and looks so sweet where she reigns. I took pictures of her on one of my visits there so I always have my little doll here in New Hampshire with me. I think my Dad likes that. I believe he always remembers that Christmas party too.

I say with author Shaun McNiff,

My sense of earth angels is in keeping with the ancient idea that divinity is present in everything.

When I was a little girl I loved my dolls. My dolls were not like my stuffed animals to my thinking—but quite different. Although they were both dependent on me for care, that is where the common thread ended. My dolls were truly in need of my care—but were also in need of my teaching and guidance. I did not believe that of my animals. I felt they had great wisdom and that they were from another realm, a part of nature that was a mystery to me. therefore I rather held them in esteem believing I could learn from them and they had secrets to reveal.

—Jan, from my *Beside the Still Waters*

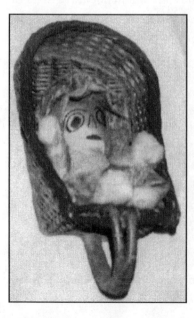

The little rag doll in a bonnet that I was given the day I visited Fletcher Works with my Dad. It hangs now, as seen in this picture, in a basket in our daughter Barbara's kitchen.

MEDITATION THREE

Friday Night Outings

The heart at rest sees a feast in everything.

—Hindu Proverb

*Mealtime is often the only chance we have of coming together and
of sharing, not food alone, but life itself.*

—Anne Scott, *Serving Fire*

Food often plays a meaningful part in memories, for special meals
we enjoy or even perhaps dislike are usually running throughout
moments and time spans that come to remembrance from earlier days
and years. Two restaurants stand out in my past and the visits there that
brought joy. I remember my Dad's humor and that he was the one who
seemed to encourage these evenings out for the three of us. They fed
our spirits as well as our bodies and that was greatly desired and needed.
Let us visit the first restaurant now. I often return in memory and enter
that door. Please come back in time with me.

Walking south on Third Street several blocks and slightly downhill,
there is a small restaurant on the right side of the street. It is in the basement of the end row home that runs horizontal to Third Street. One
never thinks of it as being in the basement, at least I never do. It is only
in relating about it now that I see it in my mind's eye and know it is so.
It is always pleasant to encounter when passing and very special to enter
its door and dine within. I remember many Friday nights throughout my
childhood and occasional ones throughout my teen years, going to this
restaurant with my parents. Each visit is a treat and each meal of mine

7

while there so delicious. I say *of mine* because I cannot say the same of what my parents order. They have an intense liking for oysters and the slippery, silky appearance of these raw oysters causes me to look away and concentrate on my own food. To see these oysters on their forks and be put into their mouths makes me shiver from head to foot. Often they too order fried oysters and the insides pop out of the crisp covering causing me repeatedly to avert my eyes to my own delicious cod fish cake or haddock or salmon. All else about these dinners at this sea-food restaurant is so pleasantly remembered, but the nights they order oysters are memories that remain in a shivery way. I do like oyster crackers however, and the waitress places a bowl of these large round crispy balls in the center of the table each time we dine there. Beside the bowl is another bowl containing horse radish. I like the hotness of this tan radish put on the large cracker, and I prepare one after another continuously as a side treat to my meal. Perhaps some have the same reaction to my eating hot horse radish as I do to my parents eating slippery oysters.

All of the comments concerning our menu choices however are insignificant to the real significance of these Friday night dinners at this little homespun local restaurant. For you see, my Mother and Dad and I are dining out together and are happy and having fun. And the most glorious miracle is we are all talking and laughing and enjoying life. My Mother's silences and absences from our existence together in our home do not exist in these precious Friday night outings. It truly is like we are *outing* the silence and absences and presenting ourselves anew each time as a loving family to our own selves and to the world around us.

> *The family meal holds the family heart, no matter how narrowly or broadly one defines "family." When those who consider themselves family eat together, harmony and healing within the group and within each individual can be supported.*
>
> —Anne Scott, *Serving Fire: Food for Thought, Body, and Soul*

The Jersey Shore

I will remember him in the ocean, teaching me how to ride waves into shore,
or swim straight toward them so I could slide down their backs
and make it out to calmer waters.

—Patti Davis, *The Long Goodbye*

Today I am dreaming about happy days when I am younger and my parents and I go to the Jersey shore in Ocean City. They are such magical days and I become that little girl again just in reminiscing. Daddy and I always go in the ocean together and jump waves and he tries to teach me to swim. He and I build the most wonderful sand castles and together we dribble the wet sand on top of the castles and this makes them so beautiful. It is at these times on the beach that my Daddy is free to be and in removing his shirt he reveals two tattoos, one on each arm. He has these put on as an older teenager and now as a Daddy he is embarrassed by them. It is only at the beach with Mother and me that he feels uninhibited by them and carefree among strangers. But in all his years he always wears nice shirts with sleeves fully down when dressed or in a suit or partially folded up when casual. Never did I ever see him wear a polo shirt, though of course I see him in his undershirt on occasion in the privacy of our home. The tattoos do not matter to me, but they do to him.

My Mother usually sits on the beach and does not come in the ocean much. She has a striped folding chair she often reclines in too. In more recent years as I look back on these precious days together I write two poems in the 1990s remembering and reliving the enchantment of sharing such times with my Daddy. This latter of the two is written with great love on the 20th anniversary of his entering Heaven on August 21, 1997. I never forget these days. Never!

At Ocean City in My Childhood

I am the spray of the ocean
   falling on father and daughter—
Standing hand and hand on the sand
   in the breaking splashing water.

I am the foam of the ocean
   lacing ankles and shore—
Retreating then back to the sea,
   returning to them once more.

I am the salty scent of the ocean
   the scent they shall never forget—
Little curly head child—sun-tanned father,
   so delightfully and completely wet.

Written with love   Jan
for my Dad
Ellis George Gray

We walk the boardwalk at night and see all of the people walking too, and sometimes I get little treats like soft custard on a cone. We stand with others too and watch the waves crash on the beaches below the boardwalk as we lean on the railing or sit on a bench facing out to sea. At high tide we often feel the soft spray as the sea crashes and curls below us and rushes under the boardwalk.

Sometimes we go into the stores that line the boardwalk and face out to sea. Often we go to a movie too. There are four movie theaters on the boardwalk. Those are happy times when I am little. I do not have to practice the piano when we are away, but when I come home I have to get back to work. My Daddy is so lighthearted and happy by the ocean and he and I get very tan. These are our happiest days., He is a precious "Daddy" to a little girl and I always think of him with such deep love.

It is said in order to give the greatest assurance and comfort to one who is dying, we need to let him know that a part of us will die as well in his death and this part of us will go with him as he travels. He will receive a certain peace then knowing he will not be alone. Too, our loved one will live on in us. I know this to be true. I did not say this to my Dad before he left because I did not expect him to go for years. But I know he knew, and prayer and loving conversation is an eternal connection between this world and the next and those who love. My Dad and I are forever connected.

> *The child who stood beside him in the ocean holding his hand and squealing when a fish swam between her legs—she will clutch his hand again,—trusting if he is with her, she won't drown.*
>
> —Patti Davis, *The Long Goodbye*

But Rochester and I knew *before* the moments that would take Rochester physically from me, and that assurance of eternal oneness with Rochester existed *before* he passed.

MEDITATION FIVE

Fears

My Daddy was pleasant with everyone.

—Janny

When I was a little girl and for as long as I can remember while living in my childhood home, my Mother would not allow herself or me to enter into our home if we had been out at night together with my Father. When the three of us had been out together my Father first had to perform a little ritual. Whether we arrived home by the back door or the front door, it was my Dad who would go in at first. At the back door my Mother and I would stand outside the door in the basement area waiting. If it had been decided we were to enter the front door, my Mother and I would stand in the tiny, enclosed inner vestibule. My Mother would insist that my Dad go all through our entire home room by room, closet by closet, examining everything to make sure there was no burglar. Not only did he check every room and closet, but he had instructions to look under every bed. Any conceivable area that a person could conceal himself, my Dad would check out before returning to the door where my Mother and I stood. When he would smile, that was the all clear signal that we too could come in.

In my heart, however, it did not always matter that my Father had checked the entire home, even though I loved him very much and trusted him. I was only a little child and the nagging doubt often entered my mind that he had missed a closet or neglected to look under a bed. Surely he must have been tired of having to go through this procedure every time we three returned home together. Maybe he was confident everything was fine and he just did a hasty room to room check to please my Mother. And so fear crept into my innocence and I would imagine at times someone hiding in my closet and I would cry to myself and sit in my room not knowing what to do. Often I would go quietly to my Daddy and ask him to come open my closet doors with me. He never got angry. He understood.

Many times I would envision someone under my bed and would spend fearful times over this. I would leap into my bed so the alleged intruder could not grab my ankles and I would lie in bed in fear and quiet so I would not bother him. Even though I was usually tucked into bed as a little one, the fear did not always leave once I was left alone in the room and the lights were out.

As I grew a bit older some of these fears diminished and only came occasionally. For years whenever I was sent upstairs for any reason in the evening, I had to turn the hall light on for the top of the stairs by the switch at the bottom before I would ascend. Upon entering a room immediately my hand went to the light switch.

In recent months I have twice seen reruns of a remarkable skit on TV done by the late Gilda Radner, someone we admire for her great talent, humor and gentleness. It was as if I was reliving my past, for Gilda's role was that of a little girl having been put to bed, the lights turned out, and she is alone with her fears. All the things I ever imagined and more seemed to happen to Gilda, and even the repeated calls to her parents brought her no satisfaction. Her bed moved up and down, later people came out from underneath it, and other frightening images continually appeared in her room. While the skit is hilarious and Gilda is remarkable in her child role wearing a little night cap and gown, my inner child could identify with "the child Gilda". It helps to laugh now at such exceptionally done scenes and portrayals also of childhood fears, but this skit does reach back like a giant hand and firmly grabs my heart. And though Gilda makes me laugh I am also experiencing her fear.

All of these things I am sharing here with you were written in some form or other in childhood diaries, for writing helped me to cope. Sometimes it brought understanding, often tears. But I felt like I was capturing my life, that it mattered.

Perhaps I should mention blackouts too, for they surely made me uneasy. The short passage that follows is from a book of mine written under a pseudonym—and tells of these.

Tonight we listened to Baby Snooks and Fibber Magee and Molly and Allen's Alley with Fred Allen. But first we listened to "The Shadow." That is the best program! Last night there was another blackout. The sirens went off and we had to pull the shades and turn out the lights for a long time 'til we heard the "all clear." It was nice though in our home because my Mother was talking and we had a pleasant time together with Daddy until we heard the siren again. But inside myself I think of what it must be like for others in Europe when it isn't pretend—and when real planes come over their homes and real bombs drop and destroy them and kill. It is so horrible!

Back entrance to 6231 N. Third St., Philadelphia, PA. Basement door (where my Dad would often enter to check the house) and steps leading up to the kitchen door. This picture was taken in 2007 when we revisited 6231 in Philadelphia.

MEDITATION SIX

Simms Restaurant

One of the oddest things in life, I think, is the things one remembers.

—Agatha Christie

I would like to take you now to the second restaurant I remember.

Several years ago shortly before the passing of my little Rochester I am perusing a favorite book of mine read many times before. Suddenly I have a memory that is so clear that it is almost like a vision. Perhaps it is one. I pause to let it continue. I do not remember what causes it in my reading or if reading even is the cause. I close my eyes. Suddenly this vision is so clear. I am sitting in Simms Restaurant on the boardwalk in Ocean City, New Jersey and I am a teenager.

I am extremely suntanned and can feel how energized I feel after being on the beach and in the ocean all day. I seem to be dressed in white, or at least a white sweater. I am having my favorite meal in Simms. I am enjoying their incredibly delicious crab cakes with white sauce and mashed potatoes. My teenage heart sighs, "This is to die for!" Oh, I love this meal at Simms so much! Always I get this same dinner after we stand in a long line on the boardwalk waiting to be seated in the restaurant.

My dark hair is pulled back in a ponytail. I can sense how good my skin feels for I have been outdoors all day. Now I am dressed in soft clothes and having dinner. I seem to be alone, yet I have never before eaten here alone. The crab cakes and white sauce and mound of mashed potatoes are exquisitely soft and beautiful in appearance. There is a low hum of conversation all about me like a subtle song.

I can hear the ocean pounding outside the open window and the fragrance of the salt air merges with the aroma of delicious foods. People are walking up and down the boardwalk. It is the loveliest vision. What does it all mean?

I sit at the little table in the crowded restaurant with my appetizing plate of crab cakes covered in creamy white sauce with the round mound of mashed potatoes. I sense I am caught in a long ago moment of time.

That I am alone and not with my parents, or with only my Dad, speaks of it as being an other-dimensional occurrence. I have never eaten in Simms alone. I never eat in any restaurant solitarily until 1986. It is a fear I carry for years until it is slowly overcome here in New Hampshire when Rochester and I make a retreat together in our cottage. With his tiny kitten presence and my prayers, I go out and visit a local restaurant alone for the first time in my life.

As the years pass and I begin to experience touches from Rochester in many forms after his passing, I come to believe this lovely vision from my girlhood is a gift from my Dad. He and I especially enjoy all there is to relish in those yearly summer visits to the sea and beaches and boardwalk of Ocean City. It truly is when we are happiest. A photo I have shows us so darkly tan we do not seem to be ourselves but of another race and country. I think we *are* in a different dimension or corridor in that magic land of sand and surf, being spiritually fed joy and peace to sustain us in our unusually difficult years.

The solace of experiencing such lovely moments in Simms is indescribable, and the gratitude for reliving a flash of one's past in slightly surreal form fills my surprised heart.

REVERIE

A scene from the past
Appears in reverie—
I am taking repast
On boardwalk by the sea.

In restaurant of old
I sit as before—
And watch episode unfold
As enchanting timeless lore.

Such mysteries are vast
That memories revive
And moments from the past
Become surrealistically alive.

Jan
February 14 2002

Silence

Silence also came from my Dad's side of the family though my Dad never used silence. He was my friend throughout the long periods of silence within our home. In all my growing up years I never knew my Dad's parents. I asked about them occasionally when I was little and then stopped. The answers I received are blocked from my memory.

On the evening of our wedding Bob and I are standing in the reception line greeting so many guests. Suddenly a woman is before me, and in only these words she greets me, *"Hello Janice, I'm your grandmother."* And then suddenly she is gone. She disappears! It is a moment I always remember. Even my Dad's reaction to this is blocked from my memory or if he even sees her. I cannot remember what she looks like, nor have I ever seen a picture of her or my grandfather.

This incident is recorded in my diary but I never write about it in a poem, nor do I recall speaking about it further except to Bob and my parents. I feel certain I tell my children about it years later but for reasons I do not know, I let it rest after it happens. I write about it only once previous to this about five or six years ago in my book *The Enchantment of Writing*, as I do about my childhood fears, and now in this book too, because it seems appropriate to include in a book about my father. At some point long after, I know my Dad and his brother make it possible financially for their Mother to be cared for in a fine nursing home. This is not disclosed or discussed, only made mention of when it initially takes place. Perhaps now I will write about it in my journal. Because it comes to mind for the first time in years through writing here about my Dad, perhaps it is a sign to explore it in writing. This is an example of what happens when we put pen to paper.,

I will never truly know or understand this mystery in my Dad's life and there is no one living who can tell me. One thing I do know. My Dad was a man of honor and I have never questioned "why" but accept how he wishes to live his life. That he is protecting his own family is how I always choose to view it. Now that I am older I trust his decision even more deeply, for I have lived and continue to live through unusual experiences of my own, and wish for his strength and wisdom—and too, his protection. In more recent years I believe that I have all three as I did when he was on earth.

*My Dad Ellis and I
the night I married—
leaving for the church—
on front top step of our
home on Third Street
in Philadelphia.
My Mother insisted I
wear her fur jacket.
It was NOT real fur!
Even as a young girl,
I would never wear real
fur!! I loved animals
always!!!*

MEDITATION EIGHT

Places of the Heart: Ocean City, Olney and San Diego

Maybe there are only three kinds of stories:
The stories we live,
The stories we tell,
And the stories that help our souls
Fly up towards the greater light.

—Unknown

My Dad is not a travelling man at all during my growing up years and even after, and though he does later take numerous trips to several other states and a tour to Alaska with my Mother and Uncle, he mainly remains at 6231 and then too throughout his retirement. He continues to only visit Ocean City, New Jersey for any short summer vacations and I am with my parents at these times until I am an older teen. It is then I begin to go to Ocean City with several girlfriends my own age and these are all exciting times to young teens, to be on the boardwalk each night and sunning on the beach each day. We stay in a nice rooming house that my parents discover and approve of and too, they stay in at times themselves when I am not there. The woman who runs it is rather a mother figure to us when we girls are there alone.

It is after Bob and I move to San Diego and I am away from home on a permanent basis for a while that we encourage my parents to come

to visit us and promise them a lovely vacation. They agree to visit and are also anxious to see me since I am expecting.

Actually both sets of parents visit us during this period but at separate times. Not only do we show them all the beauty we possibly can in San Diego (there is so much beauty!) and places of interest, but we take them up the coast to Los Angeles and they see many sights there including visits to Hollywood, Knott's Berry Farm and too, a boat trip out to Catalina Island. In San Diego the glorious Pacific Ocean and white beaches are at the end of our street where we live in Ocean Beach in a second floor apartment at 2043 Sunset Cliffs Boulevard, and my Dad enjoys the beauty there of sea and surf as he does in Ocean City, by the Atlantic Ocean. This visit includes their first time in an airplane and flying coast to coast twice.

Shortly after my parents visit us, Bob leaves in August on the ship for Japan where he spends his Naval duty, the USS Piedmont, a huge destroyer tender and he is gone six months. Though we have a wonderful group of Naval friends in San Diego, I return at Bob's request and my parents' to Philadelphia to live once again at 6231. Because I am pregnant and the baby is due in October, everyone wants me home again. It is not my choice.

But as I look back and even while experiencing it all, these six months, though Bob is not with us, are months that my parents and I

My Dad Ellis and myself outside his home at 6231 where I grew up. I am expecting my first child (June Leslie) in a few weeks.

grow very close. My life is so extremely unusual with my Mother until the very night I marry and leave home, and now she is a different woman and Mother as she is when visiting Bob and me in San Diego. I share in a previous book, *Enchantment,* how she changes completely when I leave home, and through regular long distance phone calls begs forgiveness repeatedly which I give from the very first time she expresses it. She is so deeply sorry for her troubling behavior all through my growing-up years. She continues to apologize throughout the coming years not just in these first days and weeks of my marriage. I believe she has a conversion experience in these earlier days for she is a spiritual woman even before this deep change in her. Her love and devotion to us and the children ever remain until her passing away twenty-three years later and our relationship is loving and secure and she is a most devoted grandmother. I know this deep abiding conversion in her life means a much happier life for my Dad and I see the subtle and continuing changes in him, and his fun loving side too is more evident all the rest of his days.

While I am living with my parents those early six months in Olney, they share in the amazing experience of having their first grandchild not only be born but to live with them for four months. I have a terrible and long labor and both my parents take me to Temple University Hospital on Sunday, October 23rd, and not until twenty-four hours later is lovely little June Leslie Kolb born on October 24th. My parents never leave the hospital waiting room but wait to keep vigil alone together those many hours until June arrives. Even then they remain a long period afterwards before returning home. It is an era when women giving birth are permitted longer stays in the hospital, in fact it is insisted upon. And so I am in Temple almost a week and each evening during visiting hours my parents are there to see June and me.

Once home my Mother remains at home with me during the days taking time off from work for a week at the jewelry store she is manager of in downtown Philadelphia. She wants to make sure I feel secure and also that I am feeling physically well enough to be alone. From that week on I am alone daily with June, learning to be a good Mother and doing some minor household duties and also preparing dinners at night for my parents' arrival home. They are ecstatic that I am living there and they have this privilege of sharing life too with their new baby granddaughter. It is a most unusual time in their lives and mine.

There is nothing they will not do, but my Dad especially becomes seriously involved and main protector of June and me. Too, he takes pictures continually and loves doing anything for June I allow him to do beside his continuous desire to hold her or walk her in his arms around the house. He likes to carry each one of our babies when they are little on his left arm. He would fold it across his body and place their little bottoms on his arm that then becomes a chair, and with his large right hand expanded across their chests, he carries them around the house so they have the same front view he has instead of holding them upright against him, forcing them to mainly see over his shoulder. All six babies like this way of being carried and their little legs kick in delight as they laugh and greet anyone in the house watching their ride. He is a good Pop-Pop for so many reasons. This is only a very minor one.

The period I live in Olney at 6231 for six months is so memorable that it lives with me still in great detail. I come to be with my parents in a *new place* where great emotional healing continues with my Mother and myself, and too, I see it between my Dad and her, and I experience daily my Dad in an even deeper way of new more realized ways of talking and sharing together. There is not the need to be guarded due to my Mother's former ways, or stilted in conversation. We are free to be ourselves and open and loving and it is a restorative period in so many dimensions that creates the healing path Bob and I and our children continue to share with them until they both pass and go to Heaven.

Intermingled with my parents, and June and me is our sweet black Persian cat Mitzi. How I miss her when I live in San Diego, but it is right she remains with my parents, especially with my Dad. He and I are alike in our devotion to her and hers to us, though my Mother loves her too, but has different ways with her. Mitzi lies beside me every day when I am sitting holding June or writing and shares her time in the evenings between my Dad and me. She is curious about baby June but never disturbs her. Mitzi is a deep part of our lives in that period but also in the years before I left home. She is deeply loved and loves us deeply.

Mitzi—in 6231, her home—
little cat we all loved.

It makes me so happy that my Dad can now be free to just "be" and too, to allow us to see and discover new aspects of him. My parents' hearts are breaking though when June and I must leave and fly back to San Diego. I can still see them in the Philadelphia airport that evening after taking me there and while saying goodbyes. So much good and preciousness takes place in our four lives in that six month period. I am especially touched by my Dad. As if he is not sufficiently dear all my growing up years in the great and very unnatural difficulties we endure, but now it is as if he grows even more and more endearing to me as he becomes unbound. And to my Mother too, I feel sure.

Bob, June and I remain six months more on the west coast. Three months in San Diego, but that period divided by a three month span living in Bremerton, Washington while the USS Piedmont is overhauled after its journey to Japan and other countries and back. We continue to keep my Dad and Mother and Bob's parents daily updated on June's progress and our lives. I write to my parents every other day and to Bob's parents on the alternate days. We call also. All of these attentions and loving contacts are given too during the first eight months we live in San Diego before I return to 6231 for six months to give birth to June.

As we pack to leave the final time from San Diego to drive to Philadelphia, I receive a phone call that morning from my Mother. Dear little Mitzi has just passed away and my parents want me to know and prepare for this deep change before I arrive at 6231. My Dad is too heartbroken to speak and I too am devastated. I cannot fully share my feelings with Bob for he personally has no feelings in Mitzi's regard for he does not like cats having never personally known one nor does he know Mitzi. I cry and grieve often in the car as we drive east especially the earlier days of the trip, then anticipating entering 6231 and not seeing Mitzi there. My Dad treasures her and her memory and she remains forever in his heart. It is only to me, though at times perhaps to my Mother, that he ever speaks of her. Like my Dad, I come to know there are only certain ones to whom a beloved name can be spoken when it is the name of someone that you wholly and divinely and eternally love.

Animals share with us the privilege of having a soul.

—Pythagoras

MEDITATION NINE

Telephone Call

Be not forgetful to entertain strangers

—Hebrews 13:1

It is a winter afternoon in December 1955 and I am alone with my infant daughter June Leslie in my childhood home in Philadelphia. I am sitting in my favorite chair by the front window in the sun parlor having just nursed her. I look in awe at this perfect little red haired baby girl as she contentedly sleeps. Her tiny hand is wrapped around my thumb. She is only five weeks old. I turn my head and see a neighbor woman walking down the sidewalk below. Our wide street lined with attractive row homes is appealing and comforting and I imagine the woman to be going to our corner grocery store. My thoughts are interrupted by the ringing of the phone. It is disturbing because I am so content in my own little world and the warmth of baby June in my arms. I slowly stand and lay her gently in a small crib I keep here in this room and go to the dining room to answer the phone. The phone in our home is in a little white arch shaped cubicle in the wall by the basement steps. It is in the same place in each of the homes in this row. It is an attractive little cubicle and the black dial phone within it awaits me. As a teenage girl I often would sit on the basement steps as far down as the cord would allow instead of on a dining room chair to talk to my friends. I could almost close the door resting it gently on the cord, and create some privacy for myself. Now I answer the phone and stand instead in front of the little attractive cubby hole anxious to get back to baby June. A woman's voice unknown to me asks for my father. I tell her he is at work and will not be home for several hours. She asks if I will give him a message., When I reply "yes," she proceeds to emotionally tell me that Grandmother Gray has died and to please, please tell him this. She gives me her name and I reach for a stub of a pencil and ask too for her number jotting it down on a paper by the phone. I am focusing on this enormous news. Although I can call my father at work I am wondering if that is wise to do. My father's mother has just passed away. It does not seem right to tell him this news until we are face to face. Instead I call my Mother at work in her costume jewelry store, Jewel Creations, at 10th and Sansom Streets where she is the manager. Calmly I tell her what I have just learned and we agree it is better to wait to tell my Dad when he arrives home. I sit down again in the sun parlor to hold June to contemplate this enormous news I have just learned. I have no tears. I do not cry for the passing of this woman yet feel sad that a human being has died. It is like hearing of the death of a stranger, and it is always sad to learn of a death, yet it is slowly starting to overwhelm me. This is a grandmother I never knew and saw so fleetingly at my wedding that I cannot remember what she looks like. The shock of being told who she was that Friday evening in January of this year as she appeared before me in the reception line at the back of the church following our wedding ceremony, left me frozen. In recovering from the shock that night and in the months that follow I cannot even remember her face. June will never know this great grandmother or any other nor her great grandfathers.

Time passes and the house grows dark for I have not yet turned any lights on as I sit in stillness thinking. I put June again in her little crib and turn on lamps as I walk the length of the house to the kitchen to begin to prepare dinner. My parents will soon be home. After their arrival my Dad and I have a brief discussion alone. He is quiet, reflective, but shows no deeper emotion that I can detect. He goes to the phone and dials the number I have given him, and my Mother, June and I remain in the kitchen to give him privacy. We hear him hang up the receiver in a very short while. He comes to the door of the kitchen to tell us that *my* Grandmother Gray did not die. It was *his* Grandmother Gray that has passed away at a very old age. He has not seen her in years and years. I do not know when he last saw her. He does not want to discuss it any more than we already have. I ask no questions and I remember nothing more. We three sit down at the table together, I say a blessing and we quietly begin to eat. My Dad holds June is his left arm for she brings him great joy.

> *Death! what is death? There is no death;*
> *in thee it is impossible, absurd.*

—M. Rutherford

MEDITATION TEN

Synchronisms

The present moment is always full of infinite treasure.
It contains far more than you can possibly grasp.

—Jean-Pierre deCaussade (1675–1751)

For years here in our small green cottage in the woods I sit opposite a high green tri-level bookshelf built by Bob. It runs under the flight of steps that lead up to my writing room and is on the wall filled with pictures next to his recliner. I see these books on that shelf night after night and use numerous reference ones at times during the day. One book my eyes stare at over and over again is one obtained years ago but that I only decide recently it is time to read. I buy it back then because of the title and because I know the author from numerous books of his poetry I own and enjoy. This book is titled *Finding My Father—One Man's Search for Identity in Prose and Poetry* by Rod McKuen. I decide to finally read it as I come to realize I am going to write this book about my own father, and so I begin both books in the same week of October. I learn in the first line of Chapter One that he and I are both born in the same year, he in April and I in December. I also learn his book is published in August 1977, the month and year my father passes away. I am certain now there is a reason I am to read his book! It is patiently waiting there on the shelf for me to at last read. So often through past years I take it down since placing it there, the intriguing title calling to me, but I do not read. I do not know it has these two confirmations and synchronisms in the beginning of it telling me it may be my time to look within its pages.

Another synchronism occurs by the time I reach the second page of the Introduction for I learn that Gerald Ford is one of many who is adopted. He is born Leslie Lynch King Jr. on July 14, 1913 in Omaha Nebraska. This future president's parents divorce shortly after he is born. His mother remarries and her second husband Gerald Rudolph Ford, adopts her son.

When he is seventeen, young Gerald Ford finds out about his biological father. A total stranger walks into a restaurant where the young man is working and says, *"Hello, I'm your father."* These words stun me upon reading them and my eyes fill with tears, for I always remember similar words being spoken to me. How much more an impact they must have when it is a father speaking them, yet my grandmother's words leave their mark upon me all through time. And how incredible I should read and learn this information about President Gerald Ford while his body lies in state in Washington. I read and learn these facts about him in the very period of his death when I and all the world focus on him, and his life well lived is being remembered and honored. I now am in awe that he and I each know a precise moment when a significant unknown relative appears speaking almost identical introductions. He is seventeen when this stranger appears while he is doing his routine work, and I a twenty-one year old of only fifteen days and a new bride of ten minutes.

A deep trust of life often emerges when you listen to other people's stories. You realize you're not alone, you're traveling in wonderful company. Ordinary people living ordinary lives often are heroes.

—Dean Ornish, MD

MEDITATION ELEVEN

Elvis

*All sorrows can be borne if you put them into a story
or tell a story about them.*

—Isak Dinesen

When we love deeply we always keep the loved one near in spirit, at least I am that way with my loved ones. Poetry helps me. Shortly before the anniversary of my Dad's death in 1998, Bob and I are in Wal-Mart and separate to get some shopping done. That I even remember the year shows the depth of my feeling for my Dad. On the intercom music plays and suddenly I am listening to Elvis Presley singing *"I Can't Help Falling in Love With You."* It begins *"Take my hand"* and is very beautiful. Immediately my eyes well up with tears and I begin to cry and cannot stop, and have to hide my face and try to find aisles without people. It simply moves me so much. Elvis dies several days before my Dad the same year, and twenty-one years later I hear a song and burst into tears for my Dad, and yes, for Elvis too. He dies much too young. When Bob and I meet again he has no idea why I am crying. It is the anniversary of Elvis's death of August 16,1977, and he is being remembered through his music that day in Wal-Mart. And yet for me it is for my Dad too, music from an era filled with memories. But memories constantly surface and ever shall. They give no warning. My Dad is only a heartbeat away.

You see, My Dad and I view Elvis for the first time on a Sunday evening in my childhood home in Philadelphia when we are alone together watching television. This amazing young guy appears that night in1954 when I am a young girl, making his debut to the world and ever remains a star. I and my children grow up to his music, for I am always growing up. He is regarded as one of the most significant and influential entertainers of the last fifty years. His albums are in our home and listened to and even borrowed from time to time by a tall elderly "church lady" in our Methodist Church who too appreciates him and requests tapes of his music. Very especially of his beautifully sung hymns. These are favorites of mine too. One of our daughters has a large poster of him in her room. And in the end he and my Dad enter Heaven within only several days of each other. It is an unusual tie that binds and entwines loving memories through time.

AUGUST 16. 2007

I have just completed this book today and must add one more little aside. Today is the 30th anniversary of Elvis' passing and last night I saw a lovely program in his honor filmed at Graceland, with his former wife Priscilla hosting Larry King. So many details of his life were covered as TV viewers were shown around his home and the moments and objects that held meaning for Elvis in his home and lifetime were shared. It was a very tender documentary told by someone who will always love him.

In the telling I learned that Elvis' favorite recording artist was Mario Lanza. I had never heard this said before in all these years. He had all of his recordings on 45 RPM records displayed just as I too owned all of Mario Lanza's 45 RPM records. Mario too was my favorite singer for a long period and I also saw all of the movies he made, one in a theatre on the boardwalk in Ocean City, New Jersey. Mario was from Philadelphia like myself. He and his wife sadly died quite young.

As the audience viewed this program thousands of people on the eve of this date were outside Graceland keeping a candlelight prayer vigil through the night for Elvis as they have done on this date all through these past 30 years. On the 21st, in five days, it will be my Dad's 30th anniversary but only Bob and I will be remembering, I feel certain.

I realized for the first time last night but for only one letter, my Dad's and Elvis's names are so similar. My Dad's name Ellis has a second L where Elvis's bears a V. Both are unusual names.

MEDITATION TWELVE

Ellis, George, and Mysteries

Love is never lost.

—Stephen Levine, *Unattended Sorrow*

I have very limited knowledge of my Dad's family. What I share now or have written anywhere else in this book is my total knowledge. It is sad to say but true.

My Dad grew up in Philadelphia and lived with his parents and two brothers. He was the oldest son and there were seven years between each boy. His brothers, Raymond and George, eventually moved to New Jersey. My Uncle George and I had a loving relationship but I barely saw him in all his years on earth. When I did see him I always remember each encounter as a time of fun. The only exception was the last time we were with him which was filled with sadness and memories, yet he still made us smile and laugh. He just wanted us to be with him.

My Uncle Raymond I never met, or his wife and three sons, nor have I ever seen a picture of him or his family. I do not know if he resembles my Dad and Uncle George, for they resemble each other somewhat, or if he looks completely different. I do not know why I never met my Uncle Raymond. There were no exchanges with him in any form whatsoever to my knowledge when I was growing up. Since it was obvious there were problems in his regard while I was a child and teenager, I did not think it right once I was married or in the years that followed, to try and find him to meet. And then he died and I do not even clearly remember when that occurred. It would have had to be before my Uncle George passed in 1995 for it could only have been George through whom I would learn of Raymond's passing.

I have no childhood pictures of my Dad, nor did I ever see any, nor any pictures of my grandparents. The only picture, and a fine 5x7 one, of Uncle George when a man, was sent to me by his wife. It was one professionally taken, and I was and still am so appreciative. His wife reconnected us after many years and through frequent phone conversations she and I became such good friends and it was obvious she and my Uncle loved each other very much. George did not marry till he was in his late thirties. Before that he travelled frequently and as I have written, his very few visits to our home came when I was a child and he a bachelor. I remember an enormous teddy bear he brought me on one Christmas Eve visit. I thought my uncle was funny and wonderful and loved him and the laughter he brought into our home. Both he and my Dad had a very humorous and witty side to them but my uncle was not as quiet and reserved as my Dad. Perhaps my Dad was more free and funny when alone with George. I just do not know.

George and his wife Marge had a daughter. In the early 80s Bob and I were invited by my Aunt Marge to a surprise birthday party for George. Though Bob recalls meeting George's daughter there in the crowd of many people I do not. One would think a first meeting between us would be monumental, but I have no recollection of this and we were there several hours. It is so disturbing to me through the years that I cannot remember ever seeing her or talking with her.

In 1988 though younger than he, my Aunt Marge died and this broke George's heart. We were in New Hampshire when this occurred and could not attend the services in New Jersey, but I promised my uncle we would visit him when we returned. In the summer of that year we did go to be with George in Clementon, New Jersey and our daughter Jessica asked if she might go with us to meet her Great Uncle. She had just had her first baby Maxine in March and she wanted Maxine and Uncle George to meet too.

George Francis Gray (1984)
Ellis' youngest brother

We always fondly recall that day of spending time talking and taking pictures in Uncle George's home. Though more subdued he still had his sense of humor. He too was deeply saddened by the death of his dog and long time companion that occurred shortly after Marge's passing. He felt so sad and alone. His dear dog's feeding dish still sat there in view and his dog's toys scattered near it on the floor. He could not bear to put them away. I thought of this scene many times after Rochester's passing though did not think of it in the weeks immediately after it happened, for as I have written, I too have always kept Rochester's dish out and some toys of his on the little table on which he ate. I have read many times since of others who do the same.

That day we visited George he was very anxious to take the four of us to the cemetery where Marge was buried and to her grave site. The entrance to the cemetery had a large arch of some sort, I believe in black wrought iron, and I have always thought of the cemetery as being of a different culture than George's, perhaps Spanish, and I liked that. Too, I liked its name—"Gate of Heaven Cemetery" above the arch. It was a very simple, humble cemetery. After our tender visit there which meant so much to George, he took us all to lunch in his favorite restaurant. We had a lovely time and I remember that he ate vegetarian and had his reasons which I cannot remember unfortunately. This was surprising to me at the time and pleasing that he ate in this way. Actually his love for his dog could have caused this and I would guess that it did. It is interesting that we too became vegetarians, I in September 1989 on the 11th anniversary of my Mother's death, and Bob several months later. Actually for me it was one year after I had been with George but I did not remember that until some time later. After a fine lunch we again went to his home and visited awhile longer there at his request. It was the last time I was to ever see him on this earth and I am so grateful we had that precious long visit together, and in his home and the cemetery and the restaurant, all of which were his loving connections to Marge. He visited the cemetery often and he and Marge had together frequently enjoyed that restaurant.

I do not remember when I learned about Uncle George's passing but we were in New Hampshire. It was shortly after he had passed. His daughter sent me a memorial card with his picture on (the same as the 5x7 picture that Marge had sent that I framed) and the date and a poem. I was so grateful to have this and I wrote back to her. The card reads:

In Loving Memory of
George F. Gray
February 19, 1916
July 2, 1995

George's middle name is Francis. And it is unusual that both brothers had the name of George, one as a first name and the other as a middle name. It is possible my Uncle Raymond could have had it also. My Dad was named for his father Ellis, but his father had Walter for a middle name.

It is interesting there are many named George and Robert on both sides of our family, but in naming our son George Robert it was for my Dad alone and Bob. All the other Georges and Roberts are very fine and the majority of which I never knew, but those names for our son were chosen with significant intention. Though I am more than extremely fond of the name of George and to me it is the finest of fine,—I often wish we had named our son Ellis, and given him my Dad's first name since he had no son. But we have a wonderful grandson (one of many wonderful grandsons) named Robert Ellis Hudson, and he is named for his Dad and my Dad and that is so dear and significant to me. And I believe it is a fascinating synchronism that our son George lives on Ellis Street in Rhode Island. My Dad not having a son, as I explained elsewhere, is why I eventually took Gray as a middle name for my writing name to honor him. My legal middle name is still Elizabeth.

As a little girl I enjoyed teasing Dad about a tie clasp he wore with his initials E.G.G. engraved on it. Thinking I was so clever I would tell him he had EGG on his tie. He was so loving he would always laugh like I had never teased him about it before. That tie clasp is mine now and displayed in a wooden shadow box here in the cottage. My Dad and I always liked eggs but I love one very special EGG.

Shortly after my Uncle George's passing, I received a letter from his daughter and my cousin Kathy. She asked if she could come visit me so we could meet and talk. She was a single woman and a nurse working in Camden, New Jersey. I was very excited and enthusiastic and wrote back immediately. And though we planned to be together with the entirety of her visit here in our home by the lake, at night we thought she might enjoy sleeping in our daughter Jessica's and son-in-law Michael's *Hitching Post Village Inn* a short distance from us that they had bought in

1994. Since Jessica had made the trip to New Jersey to see Kathy's Dad she wanted to have Kathy stay in her Inn. We were all looking forward to Kathy's visit. From visiting with us in New Hampshire she was then moving to Florida because her Dad had passed away and there were no New Jersey ties significant enough to hold her there any longer.

Though her visit was greatly anticipated, she never came to New Hampshire and never contacted us. It was and is a mystery. I wrote immediately after her absence here to the address on her letter but to this day have never received an answer. I have to assume she is in Florida. My family on both sides is pure conundrum. So many mysteries leaving myself and my immediate family with so many unanswered questions and simply no one to ask. To my knowledge she is my only living relative if she should still be living. I did not lose them all originally to age or death. They simply were not there, people of all ages. I am sure situations like this exist in many families. But Uncle George remained throughout my life and his, and I desire to honor him now in this book along with my Dad. You would have liked George and enjoyed him!

A beautiful life that came to an end,
he died as he lived,
everyone's friend.
In our hearts
a memory will always be kept,
of one we loved
and will never forget.

—Poem that appears on memorial card
of George F. Gray

Interment
Gate of Heaven Cemetery
July 6, 1995
Clementon, New Jersey

'Til we meet in Heaven

MEDITATION THIRTEEN

His Loving Constancy and Presence

Death ends a life, but it does not end a relationship.

—from the motion picture *Never Sang For My Father*

I have had Bob or other family members laugh at me because they know I did not hear what they just told me or that my mind is somewhere else. I am looking in their direction but not really seeing. I write of other-worldly prayer times in my previous books. This goes back many years as my prayer life deepens, but repeatedly occurs in new ways since the passing of Rochester. I am different now and I begin sensing Rochester and seeing him and too, experiencing him upon me nightly and in the mornings. Combined with grieving and learning to walk this passage, my mind is often in another place. I hear things Bob does not, uncommon and curious sounds, but too, now regular sounds to me from inside the cottage and outside from the ether. One is a constant soft humming or "sawing" never completed. I seem to be in two worlds and it is quietly amazing and overwhelming. Bob does not ever hear these sounds that I wake to and hear continuously throughout the day. I ask him often. It is as if I am living here in my normal (for me) life but also a part of me is in a parallel universe.

There is a sound I hear when I first wake, not while in meditation, though I do hear it continuously through the days no matter what I am doing. It is a phenomenon that is occurring in my life after Rochester's passing. I hear a *"Heartbeat"* in the atmosphere, day and night. It continues to this very moment. It is our one heart beating in great love that

37

I hear endlessly through the years. It is a mystical gift so divine and un-fathomable! I stand on the deck and hear it through the trees and over the lake and just cry. Our (Rochester's and mine) one heartbeat within my being is one with it.

It never ceases! Never! I wake to it and it accompanies me through the days and I fall asleep to it at night. Eventually I read an amazing state-ment telling of an author's encounter with the Other Side. He writes:

> *I remember being aware of a strong pulsing like a heartbeat. But this rhyth-mic sensation seemed to be in harmony with all of the different sensations of life that were present.*
>
> —Gordon Smith from *Spirit Messenger*

I know now there is at least one other who hears a heartbeat but mine has been continuous for over five years—and beats in unison with Rochester's and my one heart. It was so confirming and exciting to me that he too referred to this as a *heartbeat*. Meditation or prayer takes me deeper and I lose track of time. My states of awareness cause time to be experienced differently. Time can seem to speed up or slow down if I am in an altered state of consciousness. This can be so for others. There are some, myself included, who can be in deep mediation for hugely extended periods only to learn afterwards they thought it to be only a very short time.

And of course, one can be meditating for a very short period yet feel when finished they had been doing so for an hour or more. While in deep prayer or meditation or even in normal fleeting moments, it is in these states that I see Rochester in hypnogogic imagery or visions, or in dreams if I have fallen asleep. Such a dream is so life-like each causes me to wake immediately, for each is a true visit from Rochester.

Bob often will say to me *"come back,"* indicating that though I am sitting there present in body, I have not heard him speaking for I was elsewhere in mind listening or focusing on something that I felt or saw.

I know in sleep too I experience contacts from Rochester and I write each one down. Many are in my recent Trilogy. But I know too, because of what has been whispered in spirit and shown to me that much of what I experience I will never be able to write down in my journals or remem-ber, for it is spoken or shown to me in my subconscious. It is a forever gift. Our beloved ones can still speak to us in this way to help us along our corridor and we are affected by it for good in our daily lives. George Anderson, a good and deeply spiritual man, helping others all over the world whom I truly respect and who helps me, writes in his book *Walking In The Garden of Souls:*

> *This the way the souls plant the seeds of hope within all of us without our realizing they have actually helped guide us. The souls want to help us without running our lives, so their suggestions whispered into our subconscious will still ring in us, whether we have actually heard them audibly or not.*

And we too can communicate to our loved ones on the other side whenever we want for they will always be listening. I do talk to Rochester throughout the days and evenings and to my Dad, and often to my Mother and Uncle. The souls are able to communicate directly to us in so many ways. I have written of this and of contacts in my own life in this book and earlier ones. I knew nothing of this before Rochester passed. His contacts began almost immediately and spontaneously and led me on this deeper path to learn all that I am able to learn and experience. When he entered my life in 1986 he began to teach me so many amazing things about animals and of the wonder and delight of our personal oneness and contemplative life here in the woods. He has never stopped teaching me.

Our loved ones are ever near in spirit guiding us along the corridor through our remaining years of our lives here. They are so happy and willing to do this for as long as it takes before they see us again and we will be together forevermore. We are never alone in our journey on the earth.

Too, we are transformed by the process of grieving. I can say from my own experience, and from inspiring words spoken by John Edward. He states it is part of who we are now and he speaks from his own personal experience. He tells us we honor the love we have for our loved ones by grieving for them and he says *"Till death do us part"* is not true! We are never separated! And we need to grieve. It is a process. And we need to learn how to communicate in a new way once a death occurs. He states there is the person you are *before* it and there is the person you are *from* it. Grief is part of who we are and it takes a lifetime. Grief is permanent and we are transformed by this process. We must adapt our life to this enormous change as we move through grief.

I have shared so many things in my books since Rochester passed of how I have experienced his contacts through varieties of happenings both in our home and in stores and when I have been outdoors in nature here in our woods. I am most blessed. And it is in prayer and meditation and praying the Rosary that he is ever with me.

In a hypnogogic imagery while in prayer not long ago, I saw Rochester as I often do. His eyes, his beautiful golden eyes were close to me and a tear dropped out as clearly as if he was in front of me on my lap. As the tear dropped it became a soft beautiful petal of a white daisy-like flower. I cried and wanted to kiss his sweet soft face.

Another hypnogogic image in the same period occurred in our writing room where we spent years together. I saw Rochester immediately upon closing my eyes just lying there looking at me. I saw too his red collar that I have worn continuously since he went to Heaven, and his silver St. Francis medal as in detail as could be. The one end of his red collar was sticking out a bit just as it always did. It was all so precious. In that same day I saw him three different times and three different ways so totally life-like in hypnogogic imagery. In one experience his little face was up so close to me and his right eye was looking deeply into me and I felt such love. I heard this sweet poem and wrote it down furiously with pen I always have with me and accompanying steno pad.

> *I touched your soul*
> *And changed your heart*
> *I entered it*
> *Just like a dart—*

Always he is in my soul.

There is a "very tiny crack" in which another world begins and ends.
—Slavko Mihalic

Attack

Let us not look back in anger or forward in fear, but around in awareness.
—James Thurber

It is a warm Saturday night of summer in the early 1970s and my Dad decides to take a walk down Third Street. It is only a block from home and across Godfrey Avenue to the corner store that sells ice cream, candy, snacks, newspapers and other miscellaneous items. It is a store I used to go to with teenage friends on our way home from high school in the afternoons to have a soda, talk and play the jukebox. It has changed hands several times since those "happy days" I fondly recall. And my life changes also in the years since.

On this specific night my Dad takes that leisurely walk to the store to get the paper and on his intended return home he stands on the corner preparing to cross. Only he knows the exact incidents that follow and he cannot fully remember. He is struck from behind with a blunt instrument of some sort to his head. He does not know if he has one attacker or two. nor before this occurs does he see anyone near-by on the sidewalks. He is rendered unconscious and falls in a heap to the cement and while in this state he is robbed of his wallet. In this period there is apparently no one who saw this attack happen and no one who is there to help him. His consciousness returns and he slowly walks home, his head bleeding and wounded from the strike.

My Mother is so alarmed by it all and my Dad totally subdued and needing attention. He is given first aid and bandaged by my Mother and then she phones us. We all are alarmed. They live in a nice neighborhood and at this period in time things like this never or rarely occur there. She needs us and we want to go as soon as we learn what has transpired.

Since we are involved actively in a healing ministry in our Methodist Church and regularly pray with people for spiritual and physical healing, we are anxious to pray with my Dad and to try to give him comfort. As we are about to leave we call and ask our Methodist Pastor to join us and we pick him up at the parsonage around the corner and head down to Third Street in the Olney section of Philadelphia where my parents wait.

Once there and after hugs for my Dad and quietly hearing the story of the attack from him, we ask if we may pray with him. Normally shy and maybe at another time not too receptive to three who wish to surround him in presence, love and prayer, he readily agrees at this moment however to our request. He is obviously shaken. We ask my Dad to sit on a chair in their dining room so that we may be closer to him than when he is sitting on the living room sofa. We three gently "lay hands" on his shoulders and his place of woundedness on his head and nearby areas to it and each softly pray words of comfort and ask Jesus to heal my Dad. A peace seems to come over him and to my Mother also sitting next to him.

We do not stay longer for he has been through enough for one evening and we feel even our presence can be stressful once our mission is complete. He will not let my Mother do more, nor let her or us report it all to the police. He just needs to heal in body, mind and spirit and he does over a period of time in his own quiet way and with ours and my Mother's continuing prayers.

It is a hurtful incident and evening to remember. He is so kind and to know he was attacked like this and could have been harmed even more seriously or even killed just draws us into quietness ourselves, and thankfulness that he survived and is healing.

MEDITATION FIFTEEN

Foods Dad Enjoyed

Strange to see how a good meal and feasting reconciles everybody.

—Samuel Pepys

When it came to food, my Dad never indicated displeasure at any food when I was growing up. He enjoyed each meal that my Mother made and that we shared. I remember lump-free mashed to perfection mashed potatoes and fresh spinach and corn, and tender pot roasts selected and cut by Mr. Weyter at his corner store just for my Mother that she served in delicious gravy. Too, macaroni and cheese so excellent, a specialty of my Mother's, and pork chops, lamb chops and wonderful potato salad in summer. I was not vegetarian then in those years and never really knew anything about the entire concept, so I enjoyed all food prepared there in 6231 and put before me even though many times we ate in silence or my Mother simply did not sit down at the table with us at all.

My Mother also made stuffed porkchops. Mr. Weyter would slice a pocket into very thick pork chops and each chop's pocket was filled with my Mother's unique bread stuffing and baked. These were especially company fare and I had her recipe and learned to make them to perfection as she did and would have them for dinner for our Navy friends in San Diego. I made them also when my Dad and Mother came to San Diego to be with us which surprised them. They really were a favorite of my Dad's along with the rest of the meal that went with them.

When I was a teen and in High School I began to make many dinners because my Mother worked and was late in getting home. I was there most days before she was and so I began dinner and she would take over once home and bring it to completion, or I would make the entire dinner. I only had a couple specialties I could create perfectly and they were really very good and my Dad always complimented me and did them justice. One was a tuna casserole I made from a recipe I discovered in a nice Cambell Soup Cookbook in the kitchen. To this day I remember how tasty it was. Also I enjoyed making mashed potatoes, sauerkraut and hot dogs. It was enjoyed by all. I could make any variety of eggs because eggs were a favorite in our home and I wanted to learn to make them properly; poached, soft-boiled, fried, scrambled and omelets. My Dad and I had a favorite way of eating soft boiled eggs. We ate them from a little egg cup peeling off a portion of the shell from the top of the egg so as to allow the spoon to gently dip out all the contents until the shell stood empty. My Mother had pretty china egg cups we used and for a number of years I had one or two of hers in my own home after she passed. No one ever ate eggs in our home, not Bob or the girls, in that particular way however, except myself and occasionally George. In recent times after the egg cups disappeared when we moved to New Hampshire, I was without an egg cup for several years and could not find one to buy. I really missed eating eggs in that way. Only a couple of months ago I realized I could use an extra salt shaker I have without its lid to serve as an egg cup. It even has a little handle. So now I am back in the business again of eating soft-boiled eggs in that manner and it is wonderful. Bob just shakes his head and smiles as he views my plate while he eats the poached eggs on potato, his favorite, that I make him. I know my Dad is enjoying my enjoyment of the eggs and my inventiveness in regard to an egg cup, especially discovering this new method while writing this book about him. I imagine he may have pointed out the empty shaker and drew me to it. My Dad and I also liked fried egg sandwiches on soft white bread! Incredible!

It was very difficult for me when I became vegetarian in 1989 to give up eating eggs, but I did so because the chickens were not treated humanely. I had done much reading. Giving up eggs that I enjoyed was more difficult than forever giving up all chicken, meat and other poultry and fish. As I got older I was having deep reservations eating meat and fish. Rochester's presence in my life was the turning point and the cause for me to learn much on this subject of cruelty to animals and vegetarianism. He was my inspiration for writing my book *Compassion for All Creatures*.

In time, Jessica raised chickens in her barn at her Inn here in New Hampshire to serve their eggs to her guests and family, and we realized that these eggs I could eat for the chickens were treated well. So after many years it was so wonderful to again be able to eat eggs. Eventually eggs came on the market, one brand here in New Hampshire as well, that came from cage-free humanely treated chickens and these can be bought in major food stores, and we have eggs regularly again at last.

Another favorite of my Dad's but of my Mother also, was cheese. Yes—a favorite in our home too! But back in the days when we lived in Pennsylvania and the children were growing up, my Dad would often appear at the door on a Saturday morning with a bag. It was always filled with delicious cheese cut into small cubes, perfect for snacking. He just loved spontaneous short visits to see the kids and me when he felt he was not interrupting. But he never interrupted! How I wish he could just drop in anytime at all in these present years. But then I do know and believe he does so frequently in spirit. On those shorter visits, aside from when he came to the house with my Mother, he would always kid me about a huge coffee cup I had with mountain people and a moose on it and the word "MAW." It is strange the silly things remembered when I wish with all my heart I could remember so many important memories. The cup would sit around with my cold coffee in because usually I would get involved in other projects in the house or with the kids, and while I drank my first cup peacefully, usually the second cup just sat till I could get back to it and was never hot like the first.

My Dad and I enjoyed the rice and tapioca puddings my Mother made also and too, her cakes—especially a delicate white cake with chocolate icing. Shared with my Dad, I keep these memories till this day and the wonderful home cooking done by my Mother. I tried to continue that same type of delicious home style cooking with my own family through the years.

I remember well too, whenever my parents came to our home for dinner in Jenkintown, my Dad was always seated next to our daughter Laurel. It began when she was tiny, for she and Dad shared the same June 2nd birthday. For many years at their party she always got ice cream or other food on him as they sat close together around the crowded table eating—and he called her "Messy Bessie." But he loved her so much and really did not care he got messy too. Years later Dad would attend Laurel's graduation from Manor Junior College in nearby Foxchase, Pennsylvania, a community near Jenkintown. A picture was taken outside by me afterward of my Dad, Mother and Uncle. It has been in two of my books. Two months later my Dad passed away, then my Uncle and then my Mother. Their last picture together. We never dreamed this would be so. Laurel wrote a beautiful poem for my Dad when he passed that sat framed on our hutch for years. In moving to New Hampshire not only was this misplaced, but Laurel's copy has since been also. I am praying for its return to either of us before this book is completed so that I may include it here.

All of this is to share another part of my Dad's life and the simple things he enjoyed which seemed to make them enjoyable to me. And to this day my favorite cereal is shredded wheat. The great Nabisco Factory used to be not far from us in our Philadelphia area. I ate that cereal over and over choosing it above others and my Dad constantly teased that I was eating hay. Just a little aside but I somehow never got tired of his teasing and connect the cereal to him. I still love breaking those big shredded wheat biscuits into the bowl and pouring on milk. It is another thing I believe he often smiles about.

> *Thank you for the food we eat,*
> *Thank you for the world so sweet;*
> *Thank you for the birds that sing*
> *Thank you God for everything.*
>
> —Children's Table Grace

Ellis George Gray, taken June 1977
(he just turned 73 on June 2,
died on Aug. 21, 1977)

MEDITATION SIXTEEN

I Am Here

The dance I dance
isn't always in step,
But you pick up the spirit
and join right in.

—Unknown

In the past several months as I write this book I have numerous visions and dreams of my dear Rochester and I immediately write them all down. Each one is such a treasure to me emphasizing and affirming his life and he is saying anew to me each time "I am here!"

The first is a dream, an incredible dream really, and I feel so blessed. I am on a boat with windows in front, a boat that seems like a ferry to me. Rows of seats are facing the front windows. I see water and beaches in the not too far distance. I am on the back row sitting quietly among other passengers. Suddenly Rochester appears through a door at my right. He jumps onto my lap overjoyed at seeing me just as I am ecstatically overjoyed at seeing him. We cuddle and I embrace him and he settles eventually into my arms on my lap. I am visibly radiating light I am so happy and he is also.

Without warning, and though seemingly impossible for I am holding him so securely, he slips from my arms and falls onto his back onto the floor. He appears stunned or worse and I feel the panic rise within me. I have known such inward panic before in his regard. Instantly I lift him to me from the floor and caress him and love and kiss him and he wakes and looks at me with his golden eyes with such love. He bounces down to the floor and runs down the left aisle to the front of the boat and then back again to me jumping into my lap once more and snuggling close where he remains. And the dream ends.

I do not know the true meaning of the dream but feel it is Rochester telling me anew he is always here and that even though it appears that he passes away, he lives! I always believe that! Always! I believe the boat is a symbol to say I too am journeying to that place I call Heaven and Rochester awaits, and in this gift of the dream he is even journeying with me and is trying to tell me it is so and we are always together. It is all beautiful and such confirmation to all I believe.

As the dream ends, I hear a song that has come to have deep meaning to me in Rochester's regard, a popular song of some years ago but now is used in a television commercial for Cruise Ships. I often have tears when the ship is on the screen and I hear the song for the words have significance, heavenly significance now. I wake while listening to this beautiful music at the completion of the dream.

The words are lovely and the song is made popular by singer Bobby Darin some years ago. I hear only a portion that I share here now.

Somewhere beyond the sea
Somewhere waitin' for me
My love stands on golden sand
And watches the ships that go sailin'

Somewhere beyond the sea
He's there watchin' for me

I've always considered song lyrics a great vehicle of communication between the spirit world and the physical one. So often spirits use them to convey thoughts and emotions—sometimes using them as a powerful postscript.

—John Edward, *Crossing Over*

Another dream I have, though this one is extremely brief, is of Rochester standing on my bed in my back bedroom that I sleep in as a young girl in my home at 6231 in Philadelphia. He is merely standing there looking at me and the dream fades and I awake. To me this speaks to me of his being with me and always mine from all time.

Dreams live in a universe free of time and space and restrictions.
Let your memory bring you gifts from your dream world.

—J. Mellick

In addition to these two dreams I have visions in these past several months. On this particular night of which I write at 9:50 PM I walk to the bathroom in our cottage from the living room, the bathroom being just beyond the kitchen. In the dimly lit hall in front of the closet and bookcase I see a flash of Rochester, his right side facing me as he heads for the bedroom door that is opposite the bath. It all happens in a moment of time and he is so life-like I want to sweep him up into my arms. In that instant or ever after there is not a doubt in the world it is him and as handsome as ever. He is as clear to me as in life. I am overjoyed! He is heading for the bedroom where he sleeps every night on my legs in life and now in recent years in spirit. I just stand there filled with joy and tears. I do not tell Bob right away but wait until the next day.

As if all of these recent appearances are not blessings enough added to many others before them recorded in my journals and previous books, I see Rochester still yet again in recent weeks.

I am sitting on the sofa in the evening with my back against the arm and my legs stretched down a portion of the length, a favorite place each night to relax. My legs are filled with Rochester's electricity and enormous vibrations and heat that are ever signifying his afterlife presence to me, a gift he gives to me following his passing for which I am eternally grateful.

Next to the TV that I am watching, I see Rochester by the striped chair here in the living room at the base of the stairs leading up to my writing room. He is standing there facing toward the living room as he always does after descending the stairs. His right side is toward me. He is perfect, just as in life. In spirit he is ever handsome. It all happens in an instant, a perfect vision, my little beloved, and all the while I feel his presence on my legs in great heat and electricity as always. He blesses me with these gifts every night and morning but on this night he allows me to see him in a moment beyond the veil, just as in times past when he stands there time and time again in life. Thank you, thank you sweet Chester.

> *The most beautiful thing we can experience is the mysterious.... He to whom this emotion is a stranger ... who can no longer pause to wonder and stand rapt in awe ... is as good as dead: his eyes are closed.*
>
> —Albert Einstein

FORETASTE

There is a connection
So alive
and in the present—
that each moment
in the now
is to allow
the foretaste
of eternity
together.

For Rochester

Jan
March 8,2004

MEDITATION SEVENTEEN

Surgery and Silence

*I turn with love my face and loving touch
to ease your sickness and give thanks for your courage.*
—Maria Glauber from *The Sick Room*

I will tell you about that sad and terrible and unforgettable day that permanently silenced my Dad and why his raised finger on the side of the bed has become engraved within me. This is his story and part of mine forever.

On February 23,1977 I sit in one of the waiting rooms of Nazareth Hospital in Philadelphia, Pennsylvania. My Mother sits next to me and though we are Protestant this is a well known and respected Catholic Hospital. It is Ash Wednesday, the first day of Lent, and most people walking about in the hospital have ashes on their foreheads. Though Lent is always very significant to us, as Methodists at this time we do not have the tradition of ashes on foreheads in our church. This does not transpire in the Methodist Church until some years later. My Mother and I sit together for hours, mostly in silence, praying for my Dad. Earlier we are in his hospital room before they take him to be operated on. He is having his larynx removed.

Even all these years later as I write that fact I well up in tears. I can feel his good nature and see his smiles as he lay on the litter and I give him a kiss goodbye. His "*See you soon, Janny*" stays with me too. It is the only name he ever calls me. It is the last time I hear his wonderful voice or hear him say my name in that way. All these years since childhood my Daddy calls me Janny. And so my Mother and I have to leave him and sit in the waiting room with our faith as a comforter and security

51

blanket, and yet too, quite fearful of the unknown. I realize that is a contradiction but it is truth. In my hand that day I hold a Rosary. This Protestant Methodist holds a Rosary! I cannot explain how comforting this tangible spiritual object is as I sit there waiting for word of my Dad. It is then I pray the Rosary for the first time for my Dad alone and for his healing. It does not seem to faze my Mother seeing me with a Rosary for she is so deep in her own prayers. I acquire an inexpensive Rosary for this very day and find it extremely comforting as I stumble through the prayers, many unfamiliar and some well known. We sit together silently for hours. Though I am concentrating on my prayers I too see people passing by us, all in their own little worlds and many wearing ashes on their foreheads in this Catholic Hospital.

The next time I see my Dad is engraved in my brain as if with a hot iron. Often the imprint still seems to be smoldering because it continues to remain alive and burning and the intensity never goes away. I walk into intensive care to see someone that looks like a creature from a horror movie. His head and neck are completely swathed and wrapped mummy style in bandages. No hair shows, he is encircled in the white wrappings. Holes are cut out for his eyes, nose and mouth and a hole in the center of the neck bandages. He looks at me with wild frightened eyes unable to speak and I think I will die on the spot. My Mother stays with him and I drive home alone crying so much I do not know how I even am able to drive. At home I become violently ill throwing up, weak and faint. I feel like life will never be the same, and it never is.

Let my closeness be my prayer for your renewal.

—M. Glauber

RANDOM REFLECTIONS
(on the day my Father had his larynx removed)

It was seventeen years ago today—
An Ash Wednesday—first day of Lent.
My Mother and I sat in an out of way—
Hospital waiting room;—and we were spent.

There was a crucifix that met my stare—
I prayed the Rosary for the first time.
Long hours later—the doctor was there.
We left to call others,—I clutched a dime.

Strangers all about—on some foreheads—ashes.
In a daze I walked—tears soaked my lashes.
Silence! —my Father's new life long penance.
On this Ash Wednesday—he began his sentence.

Written for my   Jan
Dad   February 23, 1994
Ellis George Gray
—remembering
February 23, 1977—

MEDITATION EIGHTEEN

Fasting and Prayer

*Man shall not live by bread alone, but by every word
that prceedeth out of the mouth of God.*

—Matthew 4:4 KJV

The period that followed my Dad's surgery seemed to be on another plane or place in time I had never before visited. Never!

Bob and I decide to fast for and with my Dad because he cannot eat any solids and remains in the hospital a month. All during these forty days of Lent we fast on only liquids like my Dad. He is getting some special nutritional liquids but Bob and I drink our usual milk, coffee and juices. That is my total. Bob also has liquid soups for lunch when at the office five days each week, but never soups with any solid substance in them such as potatoes or noodles or vegetables.

In the Catholic Church it is permitted to break one's fast on weekends but we do not do that. And too, we are Protestant. It is much more difficult to eat again and then resume fasting. One's body becomes adjusted to the total abstinence. Too, most people only give up one or so items of food like candy or perhaps meat (and still eat fish and poultry) so it is not difficult to resume digesting only a few items again after two days. To break a fast of long duration as we are doing requires it to be done gradually over a week or more, slowly introducing solids again almost one at a time until the body is used to solid food. That is the wise thing to do. We often do it a bit more quickly mainly on soft foods. It is difficult to totally fast at first, but after several days there is a swing, a change as I have indicated earlier and you think more clearly. Everything you see, particularly in nature, has an other-worldly cleanness and intensity of color. It is a new world within and without. Combined with deep prayer and for me journal keeping, it becomes a spiritual experience that is unique and deep. Our prayers and fasting are for the healing and health of my Dad. My Mother stays with him every single day in the hospital and we pray for her also. We feel God is using our prayers and fasting to help him and when he comes home at the end of March he has to adjust to a new life, learning to eat, to sleep in a proper position so the hole in his neck remains open, and to speak.

It is written in scripture —

> *Then was Jesus led up of the spirit into the wilderness to be tempted of the devil. And when he had fasted forty days and forty nights he was afterward an hungred.*
>
> *And when the tempter come to him, he said, If thou be the Son of God, command that these stones be made bread.*
>
> *But he answered and said, It is written, Man shall not live by bread alone, but by every word that proceedeth out of the mouth of God.*
>
> —Matthew 4:1-4 KJV

> *Silence goes hand in hand with fasting.*
>
> —Unknown

Dad is depressed and overcome with his new way of life. As I write these events now it is in Lent and in March as it was then during his recovery in 1977, and though it is thirty years later, I write this as if it is just occurring now. It is always alive and burning inside me at the mere thought of all that he had to live through and endure in this pain and oddness and abnormalcy in his existence.

All of this could have been prevented had he not smoked, something he had done since he was a teen. After I have children he never smokes in front of them but always goes outside away from their being able to see him. He tries to stop but can only do so for brief periods.

He comes home a different withdrawn person from the hospital only able to communicate by writing to us on a child's writing pad, the type that after the message is received the sheets can be lifted up and the message disappears. Around their home are notes in pen written to my Mother and occasionally we receive these too.

Writing—we cannot live without writing. Writing is so essential and imperative to me. Writing enters into my Dad's life in a new way finding significant importance for we need his communications to us. It is a frightening, sad and eerie period of his life and ours! My Dad who has been and is such a significant part of my life lost interest in his own life. To lose his true self is a deep loss to me.

He tries so hard even taking lessons to learn to speak in a new way with sounds that in no way resemble my Dad's loving and God-given voice. While struggling to overcome this experience and adjust to a different way of living he is stricken with peritonitis unexpectedly as I have written earlier. Six months after his larynx is removed at age seventy-two, he is dead at seventy-three, a man who has been active with perfect health and young in spirit and style of living. Gone in a day!

I Honor You

To you who were so brave
as to succumb—
To a procedure that could save
yet left you bound and dumb—
I honor you still—.
that you had the will to proceed—
to impede
your spoken word;
to never again be heard.
I honor your silence
suffered in the violence
of the knife.
I honor your life.

Written in remembrance   Jan
and great love for   June 24, 2001
my Dad

I Will Not Forget You

I will not forget you.

—Isaiah 49

In the late 70s songs and hymns by Rev. Carey Landry minister to me. Music simply feeds my soul then and my van I drive is like my chapel. A moving piece titled *"I Will Not Forget You,"* a quote from scripture in Isaiah 49, is a particularly haunting piece to me. So many others beside myself find this glorious. The record jacket pictures an image of a child in the Lord's Hand, for one of the lines of the song is *"I have carved you on the palm of My Hand."* (Isaiah 49:16) Soon both wooden and ceramic images of a child in His Hand are available in religious stores and even elsewhere, and a vast variety of such statues. The first one I buy is carved in wood and we give it to my Dad in 1977 when he is recovering from his very terrible operation of having his larynx removed. If anyone reading this smokes as did my Dad, I promise you that if you knew what my Dad went through and saw him as he tried to recover, you would never smoke again.

The statue we give him touches him deeply and he always keeps it close to him. When he passes away that same year, devastating us, we give the statue to our first grandchild born the next year. My Mother requests we do this. Thus began a tradition of giving such an image to each of our grandchildren as they are born, and to other babies close to us also, and even eventually to our own grown children. Often too, I give one to a friend who is ill, or for a birth gift. They come in many sizes and shapes throughout the years, and most are ceramic now. Bob and I each have one on our desks, identical except for one difference. His child holds a dove in his hand (indicating the Holy Spirit) and mine holds a tiny lamb. (for the Lamb of God) This series also has this same child holding a bunch of grapes symbolizing the Eucharist, making it a sweet gift for first communions. My little child differs from Bob's and others in one way, for mine wears an acorn cap. This is a unique touch I add when I see how an acorn cap from a small collection of acorns on my desk fits the little head of my child so perfectly. It speaks of my love of nature and living in the woods, for this child symbolizes me in His Hand.

Above all however, it daily reminds me of the very first statue like this, carved in wood, we gave as a gift to my Dad in 1977. Truly all these years like a trusting child my Dad has known the unfathomable joy of abiding in the care and loving palm of the Lord's Hand. He is an eternal resident with Chester in Heaven.

A Quiet Man

My father was a quiet man
He never raised his voice—
Silent hours were his pleasure
And solitude his choice.

He'd passively observe
As he'd sit amongst his kin—
And if he volunteered a word,
It usually made us grin.

I often muse upon his life
When in nineteen seventy-seven
His speech was silenced suddenly
Then he was taken to Heaven.

How strange that he who used his voice
Much less than others we knew—
Should have it taken from him,
Before his life was through.

Such suffering and woundedness—
From scalpel; —and thereafter.
He never spoke our names again—
We never heard his laughter.

His purgatory was on earth
For during all his pain—
Another illness struck him down,
In Paradise—he speaks again.

My father was a quiet man
But oh, I long to hear him—
His last words rest in my soul
Prayer only—brings me near him.

Dedicated to my father   Jan
Ellis George Gray   February 23, 1990

MEDITATION TWENTY

His Goodbye

I have carved you on the palm of My Hand.

—Isaiah 49:16

On a Saturday in August of 1977 Bob and I and our family are gone from home all day taking our son George to a camp in the Pocano Mountains, approximately two and a half hours from our home, to spend a week. We return home to learn from a phone call from my Mother that my Dad has taken ill suddenly in the morning and is transported to the hospital by ambulance. She is going through all this trauma alone of seeing him in great pain and is calling us from the hospital. We are overwhelmed by this news, and after seeing that our younger children are taken care of, we go immediately to be with her and my Dad.

My Dad is obviously in distress, but it is evident that our appearance brings him comfort. We learn that an area in his intestinal wall has ruptured that morning causing such intense pain, and now peritonitis has set in. Though I listen to the facts my Mother is quietly relating, my Mother who has never left his side, I do not understand their full implication. I stand next to my Dad as does Bob and simply try to comfort him with words of caring and love. It is so obvious from his eyes that our presence is extremely nourishing to him. With all my heart I believe he is getting proper care, and if he just rests he will soon be well and home again soon.

So as not to tire him we do not stay long. The metal sides are up on his bed and it is difficult to try and kiss him, but I do. It seems unusually important.

Bob and I walk from the room into the hall and just outside the door I swing around to say goodbye one more time and to see his face. When I turn his right hand is resting on the raised bar at the right side of his bed. He slowly and with effort extends one finger, his index finger, to indicate a good=bye, and his eyes stare at me while he attempts a smile. In that instant time stands still, and that image of my Dad becomes engraved and frozen into my memory. I cannot explain the impact on me and yet at the instant it occurs I do not understand why. Even as I write it anew here and read it I dissolve into tears.

We go home. Later I know why that moment of seeing my Dad give his loving gesture of good=bye is so surreal.

I believe God on occasion allows such moments in time that remain gifts to us for the rest of our lives, even though they may bring tears with each remembrance of them. This is no ordinary scene. It is a suspension in time meant to be carried in my mind and heart. It is there so vividly today as it was that August Saturday evening in Germantown Hospital in the City of Philadelphia.

Each of us may receive one such experience, or perhaps several, but when they come we know there are other dimensions and that we often cross into places that we may only visit for a second and yet the experience remains with us a lifetime. This gift to me has been both a deep sadness and a great blessing, and I am extremely grateful for it.

Such moments cannot be contrived, but are received as a grace of God. We can pray that we are open to them for they come unexpected. This one given to me has remained a connection with my Dad that is a living point in time, just as if it is occurring in the present. I believe it is and will ever continue to do so.

His eyes and pointed finger spoke such love that his voice was not needed. Had it been it would never have been heard for he had had his larynx removed and his voice silenced six months previous to this evening. That is why his slowly raised finger pierced my heart and soul, for it spoke the volumes of love we had shared in our lifetime together. Like the saying *"the finger of God having writ—moves on"*—and so it was with my Dad.

I still cry. Perhaps it will always be so. It simply does not heal. May we meet in Heaven.

FAREWELL

The last time I saw him
So ill and so pale—
He lay in a bed
Confined by a rail.

I kissed him then gently
Then walked to the door,
I glanced back to see him—
Another time more.—

Our eyes met then briefly .
On the rail lay his hand—
One finger raised weakly,
Knowing I'd understand.—

That this sent his love—
It was all he could do,
I did not know then—
What my father knew.

With that one sweet finger
He bid me goodbye.
And each time I remember
I sit down and cry.

Dedicated to
my father
Ellis George Gray
Died August 21, 1977
(14th anniversary)

Jan
August 21, 1991

Poustinia

The word Poustinia is Russian, meaning desert.

—Catherine deHueck Doherty, *Poustinia*

On August 20. 1977 I buy a new book titled *Poustinia* and intend to take it to New Hampshire when we leave for vacation within the next few days. I lay it on a table. Later that day a call comes from my Mother telling us my Dad is extremely ill and has been taken to the hospital. Bob and I go to the hospital and visit with my Dad. I will never, never forget my last few minutes with my Dad and what I experience when I leave, and turn to glance back at him once more. I have just shared this earlier. Our parting in the hospital is overwhelming to me. I intend coming to visit him the next day. I write a poem about it all.

At home I stay up later alone praying for my Dad in the silence of our sleeping home. I pick up my new book *Poustinia* lying on the table and open it at once at random. I open to page 190 and my eyes fall on a heading on the left page. It reads *"Poustinia in a Hospital."* I feel a rush in my heart and tears well up. I read the author's words.

I never realized that a hospital room could be a poustinia. But it is, even physically. The bed, the table, the chair—these are simple furnishings of the poustinia. In the hospital there may or may not be a bible.

The author goes on to say that reading is not important there because in this poustinia of pain and death, it is then that Christ Himself becomes the Word, the Book, and no other things are then necessary. There are seven and a half pages dedicated to the thoughts and facts of a hospital room being a poustinia and I read. I had never known I was in a poustinia six times when I gave birth to my six children. They are times of pain turned into joy, not death. The pages close with a poem written by the author Catherine deHueck Doherty just as I write poems about my Dad and the poustinia he is in.

I thought (in 1977) how amazing that God should impel me to open that book and to those precise pages and read those words.

Peacefully I continue to absorb the author's reflections envisioning my Dad lying in his hospital room and seeing again his sweet attempt to signal goodbye. Tears begin to flow and I sit in utter stillness, my eyes closed and the book in my hands.

A short period passes and I am shaken free by the ringing of the phone. I quickly answer so no one in the house will waken. It is my Mother calling to tell me that my Dad has died peacefully and is now with our Lord. I am shattered inside. I had expected him to live, and to again see him when night passes and we go to the hospital. In my numbness I ask when he died and my Mother says through her tears, "at 1 AM." This is the exact time I open the book to the pages relating to a poustinia in a hospital room and then continue to read. I believe Our Lord led me to those pages to tell my heart and soul what was happening, yet I can not accept it in reality until my Mother's call.

I never read the book again after twice reading in August and September of 1977 though it totally ministers to me. It is on our living room bookshelf here in our cottage all these years. Though I notice its white cover and the green title of Poustinia and author's name and black lettering of subtitle with three sparse trees sketched also in black, I never open it. I never loan it to anyone but see it regularly as I move and use other books near it. It is a symbol of my Dad's death.

Today I share about poustinias with you. In my earlier book *Beside the Still Waters* I share in greater length and detail about them when I also share the passing of my Dad. You can read about them in that book if you wish. I do not want to speak of poustinias any further now. This book is about my Dad and about Rochester and their relationship. Rochester too passes away in a poustinia.

We came away after my Dad's services in his Methodist Church in Pennsylvania followed by his burial, his burial that since has been blocked

from my mind though I was present. I will always remember sitting in my prayer chair the first night here in the dark under the stars, and crying and crying. I had gone to my most treasured *"poustinia"* to be alone with God in my utter sadness and sorrow, and I felt his presence so intensely in the evening breezes and the darkness filled with the gentle sounds of woods and life. It was in this poustinia I was learning to accept that my Dad was gone from me physically, but never in spirit. Again and again I retreat there both at night and in the day.

MEDITATION TWENTY-TWO

Neighborhood Nemesis

Blessed are the peacemakers

—Matthew 5:9

From my childhood and teenage bedroom, my view is of our back alley, a most unusual place. The alley is T-shaped and our home is on a short block of nine two-story row homes. We are the third house from the corner, and each home has a small fenced in back yard. Our yard has lovely grass my Dad cares for, and beautiful flowers that line the side fences that my Mother has planted and tends. Extending from the middle home of our block of nine, another alley exists creating the T. Two lines of many row homes are on this longer alley, their backs facing each other. Because we are the third home from the corner and not the fifth, I can not see all the way down the longer alley the way those who live in the centered fifth home can. My view is only a third or less of that longer alley. These homes are much smaller than ours, and have no yards with green grass. All is cement down that alley. Our small yard and the large alley are my places of play. From my back bedroom window I view my small world. Through this alley the hucksters come with their vegetables and fruit, and the horse-radish man who grinds it fresh as is needed while yelling "horse-radish" all the while, the rag man, and others too enter this alley. And too, comes a very poor black man without any legs pushing himself by rotating the wheels of his low cart with his hands. He sings gospel songs and begs, and creates such emotions in me at this early age they cannot be written. I cry for him when alone, but fear him if he suddenly appears, for I have never known an amputee, yet this poor man is totally uninhibited. He seems not to mind the gawking of children and sings loudly and calls out to us. I always run home. My Mother puts coins in his cup attached to his cart.

So many other unusual things and people are part of my world there that I have written about in my book *Enchantment*, but one woman in particular reigns in her oddity for years and years. She is an unhappy person who tries to make everyone else unhappy and she is very good at this. Her name is Elsie Wagner, and she lives in the end row home on Laveer Street whose side faces the back of our home on Third Street. There is only a narrow driveway between our two homes. Therein lies the problem in my Dad's regard, but all the younger children are afraid of her including myself. The teenagers taunt and sass her back, and the adults either engage in verbal battle or with great patience and stoicism ignore her. My Dad falls into the latter category, but my Mother and others often take her on verbally which usually rises to great volume. When this occurs a small group of various ages often assembles to observe. Neither Elsie or her opponent are ever victorious. It is just like the slow dripping of water, Elsie frequently breaks someone down to the point they must verbally retaliate.

The narrow driveway between our home and Elsie's is my Dad's problem. Each morning when he leaves for work and each night upon his arrival home, he is accosted with a barrage of crude words from Elsie as she accuses him of hitting the side stone wall of her home. He does not hit her wall and never has, but I can imagine he would like to drive into it on purpose if it was not for ruining his car. He quietly steers his car forward and backward in the narrow driveway making the crucial turn that could cause him to touch Elsie's wall. But each night he backs in with perfection to the gnawing sounds of Elsie's yelling and each morning he heads out of his garage and yard making it without incident to a background of her horrible words. She is not genteel but has a vicious vocabulary. She does all this yelling from her kitchen windows that overlook both driveways. It is rare she comes outside to yell. Perhaps she thinks she better not risk that. Too, my Dad is accused of hurting her narrow flower garden as are neighborhood children and myself.

Dad after day all through the years, my Dad takes this obscene verbal abuse from a bitter, terrible, yelling woman who has nothing better to do than verbally attack him and other neighbors. My admiration for him in this regard is enormous. It makes me so upset to hear my Dad attacked and yelled at like this. He is not afraid of her even though she is a large heavy woman. That does not keep him silent. He has taken the nobler path of no retaliation, the higher road, but it must be very difficult at times. Often he speaks of it briefly once in the house then lets it drop when he gathers himself and we have dinner. Often she attacks me with her words as a little child playing in my fenced in yard. My Mother, unlike my Dad, does not refrain from responding. Elsie also attacks the horse radish man and the poor amputee on his wheeled cart, and the huckster, the organ grinderman and his little monkey, and anyone who enters our alley. But as to my Dad, I think he is admirable, a hero, as he continually listens to these cruel words all of his life while living on Third Street. I believe this is a true example of the inner strength of my Dad and remember this often throughout the years, both in the years before his passing and to this very day.

After my Dad and Uncle and Mother enter Heaven in 1977 and 1978, the home on Third Street stays intact. Previously my Mother has some of my Uncle Elmer's furniture and belongings moved to her home and dispenses the rest to family and others in need. Bob and I are in charge of my uncle's voluminous library and make many visits to go through his books and we send many to both Temple University's and Muhlenberg College's libraries. Bob is a graduate of both, and I of Temple. My Mother insists on our taking many books of our choice also plus his separate enormous paper back library collection of mainly classics. My uncle's books share life with us to this day and are deeply enjoyed and appreciated.

After my Mother passes and time also, Bob and I and our older daughters make occasional trips down to my parents' home to begin a similar procedure of going through each room and personal belongings. Despite the sadness of these visits and despite the fact Elsie is very aware of why we come there regularly, each time we do she spews her ugly tirades at us, for no reason other than to vent while we are inside. Taking the same higher road as my Dad we do what we come to do in silence, and park out front of my parents' home on Third Street.

In 1978 as I share in a previous book, numerous unusual things occur. In July our first grandchild is born, a baby boy, to Rob and June who marry at twenty years. We still have younger children and Janna, our youngest, is only eight years and loses her grandfather at this early age just as I lose my only grandparent years before, my Mother's Mother at the age of eight. The three passings of my Dad. Mother, and Uncle affect her and her teacher tells me after the death of my Dad, the first death in Janna's life, she silently cries at times in class.

Following the birth of Stephen, our first grandchild, and my Mother meets and holds her first great grandchild, she passes away suddenly in September. In October our second daughter Laurel marries, a happy occasion that is anticipated and planned before my Mother's passing. In December for significant reasons and after long months and months of prayer for certainty, I enter the Catholic Church with many reasons for this entrance associated with my three personal losses. I am now a Methodist Catholic attending both churches daily and weekly to remain with my Methodist family and keep my roots in our Methodist Church, while the children are younger and growing. I have told elsewhere how I pray the Rosary the first time in the presence of my Mother as we together pray for my Dad when his larynx is removed. When my Mother passes I place a one decade Irish green beaded Rosary in her casket with her hidden from view to tell her in this special way I am entering the Catholic Church. I do not have time to tell her before she leaves.

And so the house at 6231 North Third Street is empty and Laurel and her new husband Bob and recently born baby boy Jesse move into it after a short period of living elsewhere. They are so happy there but in a short time history repeats itself and Bob is now the target for Elsie's tirades. Day after day, like my Dad, he takes this abuse. Like my Dad he is a very quiet shy spiritual guy and he continues to remain silent. The only difference in this situation is that in a short period Elsie begins to lessen her attacks. After a time passes she is attempting to engage Bob in conversation which he limits to as little as possible, enough just to keep peace. And then to his amazement—Elsie begins to flirt with him. The entire scene changes and a new situation develops. I feel sure my Dad is enjoying this from his new vantage point. My Mother may not be quite as advanced in acceptance, though surely at peace in Heaven. And both Bob and Laurel are taking it day by day and cautiously and with great humor as Bob becomes the target for Elsie's affections and softer remarks while Laurel takes angry caustic ones Elsie throws into her back windows. It does not restrain Elsie however, from still verbally abusing others in the alley.

When Laurel and Bob move after several years and are expecting their second child Timothy, our son-in-law Rob and June buy my home on Third Street and many new tales of love and laughter are told.

They rent the home to another family, and do not live there themselves. In time in 1987, Jessica and Michael marry and move into 6231. Their first child Maxine is born while living there before they move to New Hampshire in 1994 to the Hitching Post Village Inn that I speak of elsewhere. And so history is continually being made.

Before they leave Third Street, Michael and Jessica create a marvelous gift for me for which I am forever grateful. It is truly a precious "keeper." It is so difficult for me to realize that this home can never again be visited or entered that I ask, since they own a camcorder, if they will video tape each room in the house for me to keep for posterity. They are excited about doing it—every little corner in the house , so excited that they are inspired to do even more! They video outdoors on Third Street and too, my back alley and the nearby streets I played on. They then ride down to my T. K. Finletter Grade School and capture that on tape and down further into Philadelphia to include my Olney High School, and too, St. James Methodist Church where Bob and I married. Other little landmarks are included also and this endeavor on Michael and Jessica's part is such a work of love! How I appreciate this video! From Heaven I know my Dad does too. It is recorded for me to have forever. Yes, the video tape is a *keeper*, but above all Michael and Jessica are precious eternal *keepers*.

But somewhere in the passing of time Elsie dies and I cannot say when. She spends her entire life that I know of her existence to yelling her cruel works and obscenities. I believe my Dad endures her the longest, for at least forty-four years. Just his daily life in the presence of Elsie tells me volumes about the character and gentlemanly nature of my Dad if I were to know nothing more about him. But oh, I do! This is only a fraction of the nobleness and quiet inner strength of this man, Ellis.

TEFLON MAN

Vicious words that daily stung
Were wickedly and obscenely flung
And he let them fly all around
In the air, on the roofs, and the ground.
And they dried up and all blew away—
And never struck Ellis George Gray.

From retaliation he refrained
His silence and his dignity remained.
Deliberately ignoring her sharp wrath
He always took a higher path.

For my   Janny
dear Dad with love
June 9, 2007

Heartbeat

I know a girl who always wore her father's watch after he died.
It was silver, bulky, not very stylish, and was too big for her.
She needed it on her arm, refused to take it off.

—Patti Davis, *The Long Goodbye*

The author of the above opening lines states how her acquaintance wore her father's watch with evening dresses, jeans, gym clothes. The essence of these lines speaks of myself for I too wore a treasured over-size watch and I too needed it on my arm and refused to take it off. I wore it with everything and anything else I wore. I became a guardian, and most possessively, of an old gold watch and I do not even like gold.

It is no mystery that my Dad's large watch is a treasure to me. I have so very few items that belong to him. I wear it after his and my Mother's deaths for ten years though it is a man's watch. It means so very much to me. The poem that follows expresses this far better than I can at this moment. When it cannot be repaired, for I try to have this done, I still wear it long after. Several years. Then I put it safely away. My Dad is only a "heartbeat" away.

HEARTBEAT

For ten years after he died—with pride—
I wore my father's large watch.
And though I often cried—the watch somehow denied

His death to me. —His absence was like a dark blotch
Upon my life—and to see this watch there
Upon my wrist,—to hear its soft sound,
Was like unspoken prayer—
And comfort to me each time it was wound.
A part of him went everywhere with me
And helped to regulate my existence.
A mere touch or glance upon the face and I knew it was he
Giving his time—his love—from an unknown distance.

Then one day his watch died too!
And I knew—it was true.
I would have to go on without this blessed reminder
That had not ceased whispering since he lived;—this physical binder
Of his life to mine—
A very tangible sign—
Of this man most cherished.
His ticking watch had nourished
My soul.
Symbolic of his beating heart—it played its role.
At least I still have this lifeless gold
To hold.

Dedicated to
my Dad
Ellis George Gray
Died August 21, 1977

Jan
August 16, 1993

*What is the worth of anything
But for the happiness 'twill bring?*

—R. O. Cambridge

... and I would add also but for the love and solace and symbolism
and blessing—far more important to me.

MEDITATION TWENTY-FOUR

Angel Unaware

In 1993, sixteen years after my Dad entered Heaven I had an encounter that is still very much present to me. It is now thirty yeas since he passed away which seems absolutely impossible. I dwell in a time warp and do not experience passing time as most do. In Rochester's regard I asked God that we be allowed to live as always in the present and it has been so since 2002. Time is very different and surreal since then. Also some experiences and encounters in life like this one you will read, live as a burning entity within, without a limit of time.

I take you with me now on this outing. Perhaps you will understand. It appears also in my book *Beside the Still Waters* and I am lifting it from those pages and my heart to share anew.

Be not forgetful to entertain strangers; for thereby some have entertained angels unaware.

—Hebrews 13:2 KJV

It is a warm sunny day and I am out with my friend Ginny doing errands. Heading home and about seven miles yet from Jenkintown (PA) we see an Acme food market and drive into the lot. This is our last stop. We separate in the store and each accomplish our food shopping and meet up front as planned. Standing in the long check-out line we talk and kid around and have fun as we wait. In all this time in line I am ahead of my friend and stand facing her with my cart and the counter behind me. In all this time I have taken no notice of anyone but my friend.

As we slowly make progress toward the front I turn around for the first time. There will be room soon for me to place my groceries on the moving belt on the counter and I stop talking to pay attention to the person in front of me so I am ready to do this. Still thinking about something my friend had just said I stare at the food being placed on the counter.

And then I see them! My heart beats faster and I feel a rush within it. Tears well up in my eyes and I am transfixed. I am looking at a pair of hands placing item after item onto the counter and they are my father's hands! I could never forget them! He had strong handsome hands and I am seeing them placing item after item on the counter again and again. Item after item. I am afraid to look beyond the hands, to raise my head and look at the man's face. My heart beats and beats so I think he must hear it. I close my eyes. My cheeks are wet and I open my eyes again and look. I stare at his hands. They are my father's hands! I simply stand there not even putting my groceries on the counter. I watch his hands as they get out his money from his wallet and pay the cashier. Now I hear Ginny urge me to get my groceries on the counter. That she had not spoken to me during these unusual moments was unreal, for up until I had turned around forward we both had been talking non-stop. I place my items slowly on the counter as I watch this man move away from me pushing a cart. I simply stare. Seeing his full body for the first time he is the image of my Dad in his overcoat and hat. I am looking at the rear view of my Dad! I cannot see his face. He is my father's height.

Suddenly I turn and tell my friend that this man has my Dad's hands and that he looks like my Dad. Now I am feeling an urgency. I am losing him! She tells me to speak to him, to tell him what I am experiencing. He is nearing the door. I want to do what she suggests with all my being, but I cannot bring myself to do it. There is no explanation for my hesitancy at that moment because I want to catch him before he is gone! But I do nothing except stare and listen to my friend.

She does not understand why I do not speak to him. Nor do I. To this day I see his hands, the back of his person, and I will forever wonder if I was wrong.

Because I am always open to the supernatural I wonder if he was sent to me that I might feel his visible presence, a confirmation that he still exists, a glimpse beyond the veil for a daughter who deeply misses her father.

Perhaps I would have been comforted by stopping him and telling him why I did so. Would it have been my Dad or another who looked so very much like him? Would my Dad and I have been reunited? I will never know. But sixteen years later I still see his hands. Again, his hands holding significance. Maybe I could have been more certain had I seen his right hand more closely, the one that had rested on the rail of his hospital bed that night of August 20, 1977 saying goodbye. But I was only close to his left hand in the check-out line.

This was still yet another gift from God, a momentary occurrence allowing me to feel an overwhelming presence of my Dad. That in itself was the perfect gift and perhaps the wonder of it all was all sufficient. Perhaps knowing for certain would not have been the ultimate. I do not know the answer. I am simply grateful for the experience. For a few moments I was given my Father's real presence through this man. Like receiving the Real Presence of Christ through the Bread and Wine in Communion, I received the presence of my Dad through a human being or Angel. This was a spiritual communion.

This writer too, whose words I leave below, felt she saw her Dad, the only difference being her Dad was in a wheel chair. I experienced her emotions then when seeing my Dad and again when I read her words in the present in her book fourteen years after the incident in the Acme food market. I too wanted my Dad to speak. He would have said "Hi Janny."

From behind, I saw him in a wheelchair, hunched down, with his corn silk hair and his exposed vulnerable neck. I started to walk very fast. I wanted to see his face one more time. I wanted him to look at me and say, "Hello, sweetheart, Howareya?"

—Geneen Roth, *The Craggy Hole in My Heart and the Cat Who Fixed It*

MEDITATION TWENTY-FIVE

Dad Visits

To live in hearts we leave behind, is not to die.

—Thomas Campbell

Who can say where we will meet God, Jesus, Angels or any beloved one now in Heaven. Just as we are to find Christ in everyone and treat them lovingly and accordingly, so may we occasionally find a loved one we desperately miss momentarily comforting us in ways mysterious.

Several years before this encounter written about in the previous meditation I have a vivid dream about my Dad. It is so unusually real to me, a type dream that I am not accustomed to having regularly until after Rochester passes. I write about it and record it forever on the pages of my journal, but then too, I write a poem. The poem flows out from me more readily than the journal entry and in much more detail and emotion. It seems to be already composed and waiting to come forth or perhaps it is being expressed in the moment as I begin to write. I cannot tell in which form it is being given but I capture it all at once and then stop. Like the dream itself I believe it is a gift so that I can never lose the memory of that dream. Always write or you lose precious treasures you may never again retrieve. Like the encounter in the Acme so surreal that it is alive in my heart and memory forever, so is this dream such an encounter only in another world. They seem to belong close together in my telling of them. I pray my Dad will always continue to make such appearances and I will always record them. May you too have personal spiritual encounters in other dimensions and in real life that can help you in your personal walk. Appreciate them and claim them and record them and be expectant. Thank God always!

NIGHT VISITOR

I saw my Father in a dream—
Defined and clear,—it did not seem—
This was a passing in the night—
Another world;—it was delight—
To find him there again with me—
In moment I could not foresee.

A hug and kiss was his warm greeting—
Eyes held eyes in mystical meeting—
And then he moved from this embrace,
And gently walking slow of pace—
He turned his left profile to me—
'Twas perfect as reality.

I saw his half smile light his face—
This glance toward me sudden grace.
Dressed so fine in blue suit there—
And shirt and tie—I was aware,
It was the way I saw him last—
A memory that I've held steadfast.

And when he paused and hesitated—
I felt the silence punctuated—
By revelation that his voice—
Was muted this time now by choice.
For in the months before he died
Was tragic surgery—and we cried.

Nevermore then did he speak—
He was so ill and life was bleak.
But now I saw him—flesh so firm—
Sent to uplift me and affirm.

For I know now my Father came—
As handsome image—to proclaim—

"I live !—And though this is a dream—
You'll not forget my eyes—this gleam!
Forevermore—a veil away—
I walk with you through every day.
And even if your dream grows dim—
Trust and believe I live with Him!"

Dedicated to my   Jan
Father, Ellis George Gray   March 16, 1991
(—dream—March 14, 1991)   New Hampshire
(Died August 21, 1977)

That dream was given to me 16 years ago to the very month and it is as alive to me now in March 2007 as when I was visited by my Dad on March 14, 1991.

The blue suit mentioned in the poem is what he wore the night of his viewing and at his funeral in his Methodist Church.

As in the dream it was the left side of the man in the store that was nearest to me, his profile there waiting to be seen, but I could not glance higher than his hands.

If my encounters in the dream and in the store bring back memories of your own about a loved one, take time to reflect and record your memories in your journal if you have never done so. Perhaps in the writing more will be revealed to you. Just keep your hand moving. Journal about it more than once. Perhaps you will write a poem about your loved one.

While we soon forget most dreams, dream visitations seem to engage our waking attention and are remembered in great detail long after they have happened. Unlike ordinary dreams, direct contact dreams rarely require analysis. Their meaning is nearly literal or at least fairly obvious. Their essential message is generally brief "I love you."

—from *Love Beyond Life*
by Joel Martin—Patricia Romanowski

MEDITATION TWENTY-SIX

Returning Home

One precious way we can return to places in our memory and to people
we loved on earth but who now reside in Heaven
is through journal writing. I have truly found this to be so.

—Jan from *The Enchantment of Writing*

Bob and I and our children have many wonderful memories, and those of visiting my parents in their row home on Third Street are fond ones. So many festive occasions take place there and very loving ordinary time of quiet visits. Overwhelming reflections too regularly frequent my mind of the months I live there with my parents both before and after the birth of June when Bob is overseas. They can not be kinder or more giving and I see my Dad in many ways I do not see him before and yet his protective ways for June and myself I recall from childhood when he is protective of me alone then as well.

The poem that follows expresses how I feel upon returning to my childhood home on June 2, 1994. It is my Dad's 90th birthday and the home has just been sold.

UPON VISITING 6231 AFTER IT HAD JUST BEEN SOLD

I drove up Third Street last week.
The attached row homes speak
To me.—The large buttonwood trees at the curb
Cause sweet memories that disturb.

I drove up Third Street.
It was no ordinary day.
In years past my Dad would greet
Us—as we made our way
Up the cement steps and walk—
To his door—and there we'd talk
And he'd welcome us in
And kiss and tease all his kin.
And my Mother would be preparing the food—
Always so excellent—always a joyful mood
Prevailed—and we'd be together for awhile.
Just thinking of it makes me smile.

No, it was no ordinary day.
With camera—leaning out the window of the car
I paused below the former home of Ellis Gray
To take last pictures from afar—
And to quietly say—
Happy Birthday,
Dad

Dedicated to my Dad   Jan
Ellis George Gray
on his 90th birthday
June 2, 1994
(died August 21, 1977)

Jessica and my little granddaughters Maxine and Renee are with me on my Dad's 90th birthday. Jessica and Michael and girls live in the home from 1987 when they marry until 1994 when they buy the Hitching Post Village Inn in Center Ossipee, New Hampshire. The Inn is twenty-five minutes from our home in East Wakefield. We are making a last visit to 6231 before we all return to New Hampshire.

I take four pictures of my childhood home that day as written about in the poem, and once back at my home in Jenkintown before leaving for New England I take several more photos of my two little granddaughters to end the roll. When the film comes back to us every picture on the roll of twenty-four are beautiful and perfect except the four I take of 6231 North Third Street. The pictures are totally blank! Not one of the four hold an image of my dear childhood home. Since I have been taking pictures for years and have marvelous photos, these blank photos are not understandable. There is no reason why they should not be beautiful. It hurts me very much that this happens, but in prayer I soon come to the conclusion that I am being told by God or my Angels that this is now the end of an era. No family members now own the home nor do we any longer. It is over.

Though I return to Pennsylvania numerous times between the end of 1994 and January 1996, and once in 2002, I never go back to 6231. We live in New Hampshire permanently eleven years now. Perhaps in order to move on in life and healing we have to close some doors. I am fortunate to have my childhood home in our family for sixteen years after my parents deaths. As I have written earlier it is loved and lived in by several of our children. Laurel and her husband and infant son Jesse move in one year after my Mother dies. Several years later they move away and Rob and June own 6231. Then with the marriage of Jessica and Michael in 1987, my parents' home again has new owners.

In Happier Times Our family visiting my parents at 6231 on Easter. (The "6231" sign is behind Bob.) Back row: Bob, Jan, June Front row: Laurel, Barbara, George, Jessica (our sixth child, Janna, was not yet born).

Now this era is over. The door of 6231 is closed. Perhaps one day I will return but I know it is not yet time to revisit.

> *It takes a heap o' livin' in a house t' make it home.*
> —E. A. Guest, *Home*

A year or two before Jessica and Michael move from 6231 to New Hampshire, they present me with a heart gift—a treasure. They hand me the numbered address sign that adorns my childhood home there since before I am born for they buy a larger numbered sign. The original is cherished. Bob does special work on it of cleaning and restoring the glass and too, inside where the 6231 numbers are housed, and also on the exterior of the glass. With a special little ceremony, we place it above the door of our small cottage here in the woods. It is there and ever will remain, though is only a "spiritual" and honorary address here from time past and remembered. Every day and evening of my life I walk through the cottage door that connects our home to the screened-in porch, and the 6231 sign above me is also a sign of my Dad's presence.

That sign too that was on the outside of his home was directly in front of the chair he always liked sitting in just inside in the sun parlor of his home. If he was sitting in his chair and you look in from the front walk outside, you would see him right above the sign. To me the sign speaks of him more than of my Mother or even of myself, and is filled with his love and energy.

Remembrance

I would like to share a story I wrote about my Dad in June of 2001. It appears in my book *Beneath the Stars and Trees—there is a place*, published in 2002. Its significance is greater now for Rochester went to Heaven at the very time my book was about to go to the printer. My publisher, Paul Clemens, so kindly held up the procedure until I could send a picture and loving eulogy to be on a separate page in the back of the book to honor Rochester and to tell of his passing. It is in each of my five books published since *Beneath*, and shall be in this one. Rochester is my Angel, you know.

I feel this account is worthy to include for the concept presented in it may help many others who grieve and miss their loved ones now in Heaven. It surely helps me and I continue its suggestion ever since for both my Rochester and my Dad. I have limited it to them with only occasional birthday cards for my Mother, for I know my nature, and a loving concept like this can very easily get out of hand in my hands. Before you know it I could be having surprise parties for my ethereal loved ones because I know with all my heart they would be there! They are always with me!

And now here is my secret, a very simple secret: It is only with the heart that one can see rightly: what is essential is invisible to the eye.

—Antoine DeSaint-Expurery from *The Little Prince.*

Today is my Dad's birthday and had he lived and not died in 1977 shortly after he turned seventy-three, he would be ninety-five years old. Because I miss him so much I continue to honor him in many ways. But today I want to do something totally different. Inspired by a movie I saw this past year titled *"Fearless,"* in which the two persons who star in it buy gifts for their dead in order to aid in their own healing (the woman for her baby who was killed, the man for his father who died), I decide to do this also. This man and woman are survivors of an horrendous plane crash in which the woman's child has been a victim. Having escaped death, now they are trying to help each other survive life in the aftermath trauma they are experiencing. Together they shop, and today I too shop.

After Mass we drive to a Rite Aid store on Route 16. When I had prayed about a gift to give my Dad while in church, instantly came the name of Larry McMurtry. This author is not one I have ever read or is he in my realm of thinking, so I believe the direction has been given to me by the Holy Spirit. My Dad liked to read and he occasionally enjoyed westerns. In my mind previous to prayer, I had briefly had the thought to buy him two books. I knew now after prayer I was to get a book by this author whom I have never read but whom others enjoy immensely. As we near the store another title comes to mind, *"Travels with Charlie"* by John Steinbeck. Years before my Dad had read this book and loving it so much he gave it to Bob to read. I read it when Bob finished and that copy long ago was put on our shelf.

In RiteAid I walk directly to the paper back book section, and though there are two racks filled with books, a copy of Larry McMurtry's *Dead Man's Walk* catches my attention. That title (there is only one copy) is the only title by this author, and I find that exciting. Because there is no selection, I believe in my heart this is the very book I am being directed to buy my Dad. It was waiting for me! Once it is in my hand I feel I am accomplishing a spiritual mission, and I too remember the exact shelf at home where that copy of *Travels with Charlie* sits waiting.

In my mind while driving to RiteAid I feel impressed to also buy Dad a sketch pad or a special tool. But suddenly on a shelf before Bob and me as I begin to look for a sketch pad, is a display of Hummingbird Feeders. Instantly in complete agreement Bob and I feel this feeder is the other gift to get Dad because he enjoyed watching the birds and caring for a small garden. With some inner overpowering emotion I purchase the book and birdfeeder.

Back at our cottage I immediately take *Travels With Charlie* from the shelf, an old paperback, and inscribe both the old book and the new with words of love to my Dad. I light five candles and display the books and the birdfeeder on the long wooden table, and also our gifts to Rochester whose birthday is being celebrated still, though it is three days previous. I take pictures of this display so I will always have them to keep, and then some too, with Rochester sitting next to the books. He is fond of books and is an author himself. And my Dad would have loved Rochester in life. He knows him only from Heaven. Rochester is my angel.

Bob hangs the Hummingbird feeder out on the high wooden bar on the front deck where other feeders hang. It is up only ten minutes when Bob calls to me to hurry and see. A Hummingbird already is visiting the new feeder and drinking the red sugar nectar Bob had prepared for it. It all happens so fast I miss the bird. Incredible! We did not see any hummingbirds last year, but the year before had many. We had smaller feeders for them then, none like this fine large globe one just placed there. And now a visitor appears minutes after the new feeder is placed outdoors!

I tell Bob it is the spirit of my Dad, coming in the form of a Hummingbird to greet us, and to thank us on his birthday. Minutes later the tiny wisp of a bird returns and I see this remarkable miniature creature in all his beauty. He flutters to each opening in the feeder and stays in our company. The feeder and its spiritual visitor are so precious and meaningful to me, and cause me to feel my Dad's presence.

The two books I carry upstairs to my lovely writing room and place them in view on a white chest. They are his and I say prayers over them. If anyone should want to read them while they stay here in this room on Higher Ground, that would complete the intention of these gifts. My Dad likes to share his books. And as I leave and descend the final stairs into the living room, Bob awaits and tells me he will borrow my Dad's *Dead Man's Walk* for he has never read this author. Synchronicity again—for I am planning to do the same. I sense Dad's smile upon us for his new two volume library.

The next day I have a desire to make a sketch of the feeder, the gift for my Dad and the birds. There are several colorful pictures of it on the carton and I sketch one. I am not very good at sketching spheres, but after much erasure I believe I have drawn it as good as it will ever be. My colored pencil has filled in the brilliant red of the fluid within the globe but cannot match the radiant globe of nectar that sparkles out on the deck in the sunlight. A little Hummingbird puts his long beak into the yellow sculptured flowers around the base of the real feeder. We watch him. It suggests on the carton in the information given to put a trumpet bloom of some sort into the yellow plastic flowers and it will be even more an attraction to the Hummingbirds. I have done that and replace them when they fall.

After drawing the globe for my own enjoyment and gluing it into my large nature journal I begin reading anew the information on the carton to add to our knowledge of Hummingbirds. I already know it is the smallest bird in North America, but Bob and I do not know that this tiny bird can fly backwards and upside down. Many times we have seen them fly sideways, and Sunday we watched them hover as well.

The smallest Hummingbird, the 2 1/4 inch Cuban Bee, weighs only two grams! The largest Hummingbird, the 8–12-inch-long Patagonia, weighs less than an ounce. I am inspired to read about them and learn even more in the tiny print on the carton. The Hummingbird's wings beat over seventy-five times a second! Hummingbirds have an incredibly high metabolic rate and consume 1 1/2 times their weight in food each day. Imagine! And the male is the only Hummingbird with streaked throat feathers. There is a type with more green coloring and also the ruby throated. They are such a gift to have here.

Upon reading this information I write in my journal and remember then I wrote a poem about Hummingbirds several years ago after Bob made a number of feeders for them out of small plastic bottles. I find it amongst my poems and begin to read. It seems new to me and I barely remember it.

I find it interesting the poem written years earlier, was in the same period as in the present when we purchased the feeder. The poem is written two days previous to my Dad's birthday and one day after Rochester's

What a thrill today to again see a little Hummingbird come to the new feeder. I do not know if it was the same Hummingbird that came twice today or a different one each time. Bob claims they were different ones yesterday because he saw green on one that he did not see on the other. Today the second one feeds long, then flies to our big front windows as we watch. He flutters there up close to the glass as if to greet us. It moves me deeply and I again murmur to Bob that I feel it is the spirit of my Dad indicating "thank you" for the gifts we bought him yesterday.

But I share these happenings not to just speak about Hummingbirds, but to speak also about those we love and who are in another realm. Buying gifts for my Dad is heartwarming and the gifts bring his presence closer. I have not shopped for my Dad in years and in doing this it truly helps me. I feel like the child again who surprises him, or the teenager, or the grown daughter who with my family celebrates his birthday with full heart. One of our daughters, Laurel, as I have mentioned elsewhere, shares his birthdate and these combined celebrations were ones of joy. To suddenly have the sweetness of his real presence missing is overwhelming. Now through a unique celebration for those who died depicted in a very tender movie that touched out hearts, my Dad once more is permitted to receive gifts of love from us on his birthday. And I shall do this again—and again.

> *Life's journey is circular it appears. The years don't carry us away from our fathers—they return us to them.*

> —Michael Marriott

The day after I finish writing this chapter about my Dad, a synchronism occurs. In the Sunday paper is an article about an author who has written a book about the middle aged who lose parents. She claims that midlife "orphans" feel their parent's loss strongly particularly if the second parent dies close to the first. In my case my parents died one year apart. Twenty-four years later I still miss them, grieve unexpectedly at times with tears coming out of the nowhere and into the here, and I have the need to write about them often. Dozens of poems have been written for them along with much prose. I still had young children when they left, my youngest of six only eight years. This author tells how people stand at her booksignings to tell their stories of loss to her, and how after losing both parents these middle aged children truly feel "orphaned". As an only child I too experience this ever since their deaths. One person states that though she is without her parents a decade there is still an emptiness that she cannot describe. Author Jane Brooks too was overwhelmed by her mother's death, so overwhelmed by grief she worried something was wrong with her. Her father had died two years previous. The book is a result of that grief after six years and contains an exploration of her own experience as well as those of fifty-two fellow "orphans" she interviewed along with assorted grief counsellors and therapists. The name of her book is *Midlife Orphan* and one can learn more from her website also. (www.midlifeorphan.com)

Though the events in this meditation of my Dad's birthday took place when he celebrated his 95th in Heaven, the following poem is still very appropriate. Written for him when he celebrated his 89th birthday.

Happy Birthday, Dear Dad

You're eighty-nine, Dear Dad—it's true
And yet in Heaven your life is new—
And I shall never see you age—
No, never have that normal gauge—
And so envision you in ways—
We shared our lives in earlier days.

One thing I know—beyond that door—
You're just as handsome as before!
You're fun and witty—and still charming.
Do the angels find you quite disarming?

Dedicated to my Dad   Jan
Ellis George Gray
on his birthday
June 2, 1993

Eternal Moments

As I share with you in this book portions of the lives of my Dad and Rochester, I cannot omit telling of Rochester's last moments and his Eternal Gift to me, just as I have told you of my last moments with my Dad.

The meditation that follows is from my book In *Corridors of Eternal Time*. I can never re-write it anew in other words. They are sacred words given to me when I was so depleted and sad I could barely get my thoughts assembled. I cannot bear to read them and place them here by faith to possibly help others. I share them again for the first time since they appeared in *Corridors*. I believe they are meant to be in this book secure with my Dad.

The book *Corridors* is written in journal form. Though Rochester went to Heaven March 8th, I wait to write this entry below on the day after his birthday. I began the book when he passed, but could not write of all that transpired in this meditation then. This is only the evening portion of the entry. The earlier part of the day is recorded in my journal *Corridors* also

> *It seems I have no tears left. They should have fallen —*
> *Their ghosts, if tears have ghosts, did fall—that day.*
>
> —Edward Thomas from *Tears*

FRIDAY EVENING, MAY 31, 2002

We walked into that Veterinarian's clinic at 5 PM on Friday, March 8th, and were directed to one of the small rooms. The three of us entered and a woman Veterinarian was there with a young assistant. There was no conversation except the doctor's instructions to wrap Rochester in a towel provided. I felt like I was in a night mare and cannot imagine why I did not scream. I had thought yesterday while with him of we three just running away, that he would get well and what we were living through was not true. We took him from his carrier and like a robot I did what she asked not believing I was doing it. I laid him on the table and wrapped him in a tan towel like a baby. There was no time allowed. They wanted it done at once. In that moment I died a thousand deaths. I kissed him and whispered soft things to him and stood there holding him, the back of his little head against my cheek and his little paws lying over the towel. I can barely write this to tell you it is so devastating to me. I cannot see to write.

As his little head rested on me she quickly put a needle into his right paw and he was gone instantly. I do not know how I survived it. I wanted to go too. They wanted to take him from me and I said "no," that I wanted to sit and hold him awhile. Bob stood by me and I sat down cradling him in my left arm like a baby. I could barely see him for my tears but his eyes were still open and he felt so tiny in the towel. I kept kissing his little face and soaking it in tears, and holding his little paws that I had held every day and night for so many years. I was out of my mind. His little stomach moved and made a little sound. These were gasses, but I thought he was still alive. Bob assured me it was not so.

Suddenly in the midst of all this pain and grief a word popped into my head, a word at that moment that I did not know the meaning of any more than I knew my own name at that moment. The word was "Anima." Upon hearing the word mentally I instantly knew what I had to do. Bob just watched me saying nothing. Barely able to see I began to give Rochester little kisses on his mouth, and then I gently opened his tiny mouth until it was substantially opened. I then placed my lips and mouth over his open mouth totally encasing it, and began to draw in deep breaths from Rochester. I knew I would carry his breath within me always. Over and over again I drew his breath into my body and kept doing this until I knew I was to stop. I knew I was doing a deeply spiritual act yet had only been led to do it moments before.

I then kissed him and gently closed his dear little mouth and kissed his eyes and closed those too. He lay in my arms like the precious Angel he is and I just could not stop looking at him. By now my lips were tingling and felt unusual but nothing mattered but Rochester. I sat in the chair holding him while Bob asked the assistant twice when she returned to please allow us more time. I cannot write about that time with him in my arms, my final minutes of ever holding him in reality again. My heart was so broken I wanted to die. If I could have taken the needle for him I would have done that, or given him my liver. The moment came at 5:45 PM when I was forced to lay him in the arms of the assistant. As she stood in the hall with him I again wanted to snatch him and run. To part with his tiny body ripped my heart apart. I could not bear that it was my very last time to see him until we are together in Heaven. I died within seeing her turn and carry my little one away! Through my grief I asked her where she was taking him and when she replied I just turned and walked away. I was crazy inside! I wanted to die and be with him.

May no one else ever have to go through such pain. We had made arrangements for cremation but I cannot tell you when I did that. I only knew it had to be so, so that I might forever have his ashes, and then one day my ashes will be added and mixed with his, and hopefully Bob's too. We left the office and I cannot remember the drive home. It was an "hour of lead," of experiencing a death of myself.

Once in the cottage in total grief I listened to what I was feeling within—, inspired thoughts I know with a certainty. I believe Chester inspired me to draw his breath from him again and again. It had only entered my mind following the word "Anima" that had made its entrance also. I believe he inspired me to draw out his breath so that I might be a vessel and carrier of his breath to join us in the deepest way possible. Perhaps it was both God and Chester, and Mary too— and all the Angels. I am only so deeply grateful I obeyed without hesitation, acting on a word whose meaning I did not know then, and on instructions that appeared and I knew only that I was to follow, and wanted to follow with all my being.

When I looked up the word "Anima" in the dictionary the next day I was overwhelmed to learn it meant "breath, soul."

Forever I am carrying his breath and soul within me until we are to-gether again. I look at the words I have written down in my tablet when we were together in our room Thursday, March 7th. He said to me:

Thank you for holding me tomorrow, for being there. I will enter you in a way you could never dream and this bond is eternal."

He had told me what would happen but I could not understand then. I had only to obey what was being said to me within, as I stood holding his precious being in that Veterinarian's office. He trusted me to know and obey, that is how close and one we were and are! He passed on to me the greatest treasure he could ever give to me, his very breath and soul to carry for him forever. It is a gift that is so utterly divine and surprising and so cherished by me that it cannot be expressed in earthly words. I only know if I were offered all the wealth in the world it would seem ridiculous in light of the wealth I carry within. I have thought, "what if I did not obey or understand?" when that word and impulses to act were given? And then I conclude that that was not an option. After all our years together and our communication by thought and word, Rochester knew without a doubt I would know and act, even predicting it to me in his words on Thursday that I wrote down. We are so one he would not let me fail in my grief. He made it so emphatically known I acted immediately. I offer daily much thanksgiving for Rochester's eternal gift to me.

To have this happen is sacred and other worldly, but that is how I live. Life has been that way since March 8th. Life has always been that way in the presence of Rochester.

Still yet another blessing of such worth was awaiting upon our arrival home that night of March 8th, that night that seems unreal. Bob went over to his office to send several e-mails to family and to the staff at Blue Dolphin Publishing. As he went online to send the e-mail of Rochester's passing to my publisher and staff there was one awaiting him there from Blue Dolphin, from my friend Chris Comins. Chris's message stated that at 5:10 PM he had a vision of Rochester in the center of a circle of Angels and Light. He wanted to know if Rochester was alright. Rochester had passed at 5:07 PM in my arms and Chris saw him in this heavenly state at 5:10 PM, not knowing of all that was transpiring here in New Hampshire 3,000 miles from him in California. I cannot express what this vision has continued to mean to me and the peace it gives to me. I know Rochester is safely in Heaven awaiting the day we will be reunited.

This vision has sustained me since March 8th, for every night since September 1989 Chester has fallen asleep "in a ring" of etherial music titled *"The Fairy Ring."* I have written of it in an earlier entry. Fairies are deva, lower than the angels yet a form of angels, of the spiritual world. I believe the Angels cared for my little angel in the most tender of ways making his passage filled with love and memories of the countless precious nights we two spent "in The Fairy Ring," together. And soon, very soon, we shall spend every night there together again, for I still have been hesitant to listen. The cassette still sits in the tape player waiting for the night when Chester and I will forever share our music once more.

These two supernatural happenings of March 8th, my carrying now Rochester's "Anima," and his encounter with "Angels and Light" that carried him to Heaven, have been my sustaining strength in the past days and weeks since March 8th, and will be in what life I have here on earth ahead. We shall be together again forever in Heaven, and while I await I carry him within and live with his spirit.

In a previous book of mine I wrote these words about Rochester.

He is enchantment, and his presence lights up my existence! Angels do that! We share our moments and days and because of him I am a finer and better person. He is an Angel, my shining Star sent by God."

I have always believed he is an Angel. That belief can never be shaken. He has always too—been a shining Star in my life, for he has lightened my heart and soul all these past years and travelled a healing path with me. He has brightened my existence with the light and height and depth of his love. He continues to do so and always shall.

Soon after we arrived home the evening of March 8th, and after learning of the vision, in my brokenness I looked up at the night sky and knew my little one was taken in a circle of Light and Angels to God;— Rochester is my shining star, my Angel.

It seems so right to include this poem I wrote for his May 30th birthday in 1998.

MY STAR

I gaze up at the heavens
　　　and see the brilliant, shimmering stars
　　　　　in the night sky—
And in wonder feel that I
　　　am one
　　　　　with all creation.
And yet this inward elation
　　　cannot compare
　　　　　to what I feel
When I gaze upon the radiant star
　　　who shares my nights and days—
　　　　　shining his love in tender ways
　　　　　　everywhere we are!
He is my Angel of Light
　　　my one true star—
　　　　　more beauteous
　　　　　　than all the stars of night.

For Rochester　　　　　　　　　　　　　Jan
with inexpressible love
on his birthday
May 30, 1998
— and for all time —

And this night of May 31st at 5 PM I again keep my hour vigil with
him, in tears, and turning again to the Rosary and the comfort of those
repetitive prayers, I know Mary is with us. I look from time to time at
Rochester's comforter across from me on the bed. His floral tin of ashes
sits on the spread next to it. He is with me as strongly as if I could see
his blessed little body of marmalade fur on the quilt, and his golden eyes
gazing at me in love. It shall always be so.

Rochester, beloved feline companion, confidant, counsellor, and ministering angel, finished his work here after almost sixteen years (minus one month), and passed on. He was a motivator and enabler to me and unselfishly gave of himself in deep love continually. He was with me every day—all day while I wrote, since he was eight weeks old, and was my inspiration. He was with me through every night. Rochester was the Star of every book I wrote. He was most loving friend to Bob. His sudden illness diagnosed only Thursday, March 7th brought about his reluctant departure. We were with him 'til he passed—and after. He shall forever be with me in soul and spirit, to help and inspire until we are together once more.

Rochester entered Heaven
March 8, 2002
5:07 PM

MEDITATION TWENTY-NINE

The Ring

—his Masonic ring on my finger glinted in the light. It dawned on me—
for the millionth time—that I would never see his face, hear his voice again,
and I wanted to throw myself against a wall to stop the pain.
—Geneen Roth, The Craggy Hole In My Heart
and the Cat Who Fixed It

I have written elsewhere in at least two of my previous books in my Trilogy that I have asked my Dad to be Rochester's friend and guardian in Heaven. Though he did not know Rochester in this life, I feel certain he has known him and been aware of him since Rochester entered my life in 1986. My Dad had always loved our family cat Mitzi so deeply, I felt certain he would cherish my Rochester too, and care for him until I joined them. In my heart is that assurance.

Because I am continually aware of Rochester's presence in extraordinary ways, and too, in subtle ordinary ways, I ask my Dad in prayer to also communicate in some way with me. I do not realize many truths when my Dad passes away in 1977 for I have never been taught them, nor in my reading.

I experience my Dad in dreams but nothing more, except in my own thoughts, or in the poems I write for him and about him, or the writings speaking of him in my past published books. In one exceptional instance I feel I see him and write about this also in my previous book, *Beside the Still Waters*, and that encounter is written earlier in these pages. Since that particular instance I again feel I encounter him several years later and this experience is recorded elsewhere in this very book. In the first sighting of him recorded in *Beside*, I feel I am so struck by what I believe to be his presence seeing only his hand up close, and the back of his figure walking away from me, I let him go. I will never know for certain in this life, but believe it is him. My friend Ginny shares this unexpected experience with me and I believe she too is moved by it.

And so anew I pray that my Dad will show himself to me as Rochester continues to do. The day after I lift this silent petition to Jesus, an amazing incident occurs. I am in the bedroom and about to leave, when I briefly turn back to do something. In this instant an object swiftly flies off of my bureau! It comes from the back of the bureau and rises into the air at least a foot from its surface, and in a half circle speeds downward to the floor. I simply stand there as if glued to the spot and in awe! What is it? How can such a thing occur when no one is there but myself and Rochester's spirit? Over the initial shock I begin to look for the object on the carpet and find it almost under the bed. Holding it in my hand tears come, for I am cupping a treasure I have not seen in years. I thought it permanently lost and put it to rest in my mind, even though feeling terrible that I am so careless as to lose it.

In my hand is my Dad's gold Masonic ring, a rather large ring with an emblem of an eagle on it. At one point in his life he wore it regularly, then put it away when he no longer was active in this group. It becomes mine when he goes to Heaven. Now it is making a new appearance!

As I write this now I still do not know if my Dad tosses the ring up in the air to show me he is very much alive and with me, or if Rochester, sitting on my bureau as he often did, pats it vigorously into the air with his soft white paw. He did this many times with other belongings of mine in sweetness and fun. And although my bureau is not neat and tidy, I do know my Dad's ring is not upon it all these years it is missing. I keep it in a jewelry box in a bureau drawer, never carelessly loose on top of the bureau.

And how can it just reappear and be tossed in the air at that moment for me to discover after previously praying that my Dad will reveal himself to me? I do not know the answers. I am finally beginning to experience the treasures revealed from beyond. I only know it falls at my feet the day after I pray, as if it propels into the air by an unknown force. Whether it is my Dad announcing his presence or Rochester, it is all beauty, truth and consolation to me, affirming once again that our precious loved ones are ever with us.

Do not miss the subtle ways your loved ones come through. Do not look for great big things, though in this particular instance it truly is remarkable. But not every time I am blessed by Rochester's presence does he toss a ring into the air! Our sweet loved ones are trying to come through so they may show you they are there all the time! How I wish I knew this all those years after my Dad passed away. How many subtle "hellos" do I miss day after day? I believe it has taken my beloved Rochester to teach me awareness on a daily basis, and then every now and then he causes an enormous gift to be given to me from him within the walls of this cottage or elsewhere in daily life. But as to the tosser of this ring, so far it remains a mystery though I pray.

I think Rochester and my Dad are in cahoots. They both have mischievous personalities at times. But it confirms anew in my heart, though Rochester's spirit is ever with me here, my Dad and he are together in Heaven.

The quotation about another Dad's ring at the beginning of this sharing could be mine as well, and too, her despair when the author realizes for the millionth time she will never see or hear or experience her Dad again in the way she once did. I too have these depths of emotion about my Dad. Again and again and again.

And now as Geneen does, I continually wear my Dad's Masonic ring. It has enormous presence and meaning to me especially in the present as I write this book about his life. I too share Geneen's emotions.

We cannot but speak the things we have seen and heard.

—Saints Peter and John, Acts 4:20

THE MEMORY

I am the memory of a father
  drifting in and out of the mind—
    drifting through time—
      down through the years.
I am the memory of a father
  gentle and kind—
    passing in his prime—
      bringing tears.
I am the memory of a father
  carried in a heart—
    dwelling apart—
      that adheres.
I am that memory
  that shall ever live—
    that shall ever give
      love—to the one who remembers.

Written for my Dad   Jan
with love—   August 11, 1997
Ellis George Gray
for his 93rd Birthday
June 2, 1997

MEDITATION THIRTY

A Symbol of Eternal Love

Karen Pochlein wore Shelby's collar as a bracelet
for weeks after the cat's death.

—Karen Commings, *Cat Fancy*, August 1997
—*Death of a Feline Friend*

Too, another ring of love and solace to me is Rochester's red collar
that encircles my left arm forever, buckled into the same little hole
that it was when around his neck, and never, never unbuckled.

—Janice Gray Kolb, *In Corridors of Eternal Time*

The first quotation that appears in this meditation was included in a moving collection of writings concerning the deaths of beloved cat companions in an issue of Cat Fancy. It is a magazine I subscribed to for many years only finally ending the subscription last year. I had not seen the article when it appeared, but I feel certain I probably saw the title and elected not to read it. For you see, Rochester was still with me then in body and spirit and I could not have read such writings then. I never thought Rochester would pass away. Unrealistic thinking, but it was so.

After he did pass, my childhood friend Lois who has two marmalade cat companions of her own, sent me the article. It was only then I could read it and have read it many times since, and will again.

The woman whom I have quoted wore her cat's collar for weeks after his death. When I read that it touched me so deeply and I cried for I had already been wearing Rochester's collar too for weeks. Now it is five years, three months and five days I have been wearing it—and I always shall.

Please—let me tell you our story.

A Circle of Eternal Love

St. Francis etched in finest pewter
On the round tag at his neck
Does bedeck—and yes, protect —
The life of my dear feline suitor.

A red heart, too, has name and number —
Symbolic of the Sacred Heart —
And when in play or deepest slumber —
God's with my precious counterpart.

Saturday, March 9, 2002

I left my beloved Rochester with a woman I did not know and came home instead with only his collar. I slipped it on my arm under my sweater to keep it safe on that drive home that I do not remember. I could not see on the drive home.

Picture of Rochester's red collar covered in black, star-studded material with our book, Compassion, *and his handsome picture on the cover.*

At home the little pewter St. Francis medal and red metal heart with his veterinarian information on jangled each time I moved my arm. There is a tiny bell on it too. They are attached to the new purple nylon collar we had put on him only five weeks or so ago. He looked so handsome in it, but looked even more handsome with no collar, as he does on the cover of my book *"Compassion For All Creatures."* He is so beautiful on the cover of that book. When I would walk in Bookland, my favorite bookstore in Sanford, Maine and see copies of this book displayed in various places, my heart would melt. To think that my little beloved was there for all to see. So many commented on the beauty of that cover there. His eyes look right at me. I used to stand and stare in their store window where many copies of *"Compassion"* appeared for many weeks displayed beautifully by my friend Cheryl who worked in Bookland, a friend I had come to know by shopping there and through my books. To think that my precious Rochester was in this store window (and other windows elsewhere) made me feel such gratitude and love for him. It was his book. All my books are his.

This day after his leaving I get out his previous collar from my drawer. I have each one he has ever worn. Though he remained indoors for his safety's sake, he still wore a collar on the chance he ever slipped out. But he did not try to do that. His previous collar is red and soft. I had carefully printed his name and phone number on it but it had almost worn off, though can still be read. He had worn this soft collar for several years and it looked attractive against the white fur at his neck. It too had had the same St. Francis medal upon it and red heart, until we transferred them to the purple collar. I held it in my hand crying and then kissed it. I removed the purple collar slipping it over my hand, not unhooking it. Saying a prayer for my little Chester I slipped the red one over my left hand and onto my wrist. It was loose but could not fall off. I wanted it to remain hooked in the same hole on the collar as it had been when around Rochester, just as the purple one shall remain hooked. Forever hooked, it was a never ending circle symbolizing eternal love—the love Rochester and I share. This was the collar I would wear, the red one—not the newer one. This is the one he had worn much longer and he had it on in so many, many pictures I had taken of him.

Though I have worn other things for him through the years, a little silver cat head necklace given to me the year Chester came into my life and never removed since, a silver ring with an amethyst heart symbolizing our love, and a silver ring bearing an image of a sitting cat, this red collar was now going to be mine forever.

My left arm will indeed hold significance. On that wrist also is a silver cuff bracelet similar to those worn by many for those missing in action in Viet Nam. I began to wear this bracelet in January, obtaining it after I learned such bracelets were available for the victims of September 11th on CNN. Though names are available of Firemen, Policemen, the victims at the Pentagon and from the field in Pennsylvania where the plane crashed,—I requested a name of someone who died in the World Trade Center since that is where I saw the first planes enter that horrendous morning. My bracelet has a fine man's name on (a husband, father and grandfather), who died in The World Trade Center in the offices of Cantor-Fitzgerald. The bracelet is called a Mercy B.A.N.D. and is to be worn forever. The initials stand for "Bearing Another's Name Daily."

And so I add another band—red, next to the silver, and I too shall "bear Rochester's name daily." And when the name wears off perhaps I shall add it again. I will know what to do when the time comes. And I will wear it until he and I are reunited in Heaven.

> His little tinkling tags that dangle—
> Let me know that he is near.
> His dear approach from any angle—
> One cannot help but overhear.
>
> Ah—now he springs onto my lap—
> He cares not its the thirtieth of May—
> He snuggles down into his nap—
> I hold his paw
> and still in awe
> I celebrate his sixth birthday.

(Poem: Rochester's birthday)

Dedicated to   Jan
Rochester Harry Whittier Kolb
on his birthday—

—and now in these sad, sad days.

There are two minor changes for Rochester's and my red collar bracelet since the writing of that meditation in 2002. As time passes, the collar becomes very worn for it is not new when I first slip it on. It has Rochester's energy in it and a part of him and I am afraid I may lose it. One day while shopping in Maine, I have an inspired idea I believe to be from Rochester for several reasons. And so while there I buy a quantity of material in the sewing section of a favorite store—a store in which Rochester sends me signs and gifts that I write about in previous books since his passing.

I immediately see and know I am to buy a large black piece of material covered in gold, silver and pale green stars of various sizes. Like the black night sky and stars that hold great meaning to me in Rochester's regard, so this cloth looks like the night sky here in New Hampshire. And as I have repeatedly said and written—Rochester is my star.

The next day I neatly cover Rochester's red collar removing it from my arm for the first time. I roll it in the star studded black material and stitch it very carefully. To me it looks beautiful and I slip it on and the collar begins a new cycle. I cannot tell you when that happens for time is different in my life since Rochester passes. Perhaps two and a half years later. And then much more time passes and the black material becomes extremely worn after several years and it is time again for a new covering. Just days ago I remove the old and gently hold the dear red collar that has been secluded away and protected. I kiss it and pray anew with it and wrap it in beautiful new material of the same black star studded design. I have what now seems an endless supply. I add only one thing inside with the collar, a tiny piece of paper with a tiny phrase of love of four words in Latin. Since it is for Rochester alone, I cannot write it here. It is a phrase I read in a book of grieving and melts me on the spot.

His purple collar also remains buckled into the same hole, an eternal circle that lies on his quilt by day and my night-table by night.

—Jan, *In Corridors of Eternal Time*

A circle or ring is symbolic of endless love, the love that Rochester and I experience and have been given by God, and that is watched over and protected by Mary and the Angels

We who choose to surround ourselves with lives even more temporary than our own, live within a fragile circle, easily and often breached. Unable to accept its awful gaps, we still would live no other way. We cherish memory as the only certain immortality never fully understanding the necessary plan.

—Irving Townsend, *The Once Again Prince* from
In Corridors of Eternal Time by Jan

Rochester
January 2002

This picture was taken six weeks before he went to Heaven.
He is wearing the red collar that I now wear ever since his passing.

MEDITATION THIRTY-ONE

The Blue Dishpan

In a faded blue dishpan
Found in a closet used for storage—

—Jan, two lines from poem *From Afar*

Sometime in the early to mid-nineties I discover a small collection of my Mother's belongings in a closet on the third floor in our home in Jenkintown, Pennsylvania. After my parents sudden deaths in 1977 and 1978, these belongings are tucked away as were many other items that are theirs. I do not ever remember this particular collection of papers, envelopes and photos in an old blue dishpan however. It is a major discovery to me and most moving.

Among these personal things I find a piece of torn paper all creased and folded unevenly. It looks like trash. But unfolding it carefully I find within a treasure. I read what I discover through tears.

I never see my Mother engage in writing and I have only several tiny thank you notes from her. And her handwriting is a scribble that I can never understand without effort. Yet here before me in this hasty writing I know—is a poem. She has written a poem about me—and also about my tiny first baby. There is no date, but it has to be written while my daughter June is an infant. It has to be written within the first year of our marriage, which makes it especially meaningful. As I write elsewhere, my Mother apologizes repeatedly after I marry for her silence to me through the years, and I accept this the first time she says it. I believe this poem is a love gift from the depths of her heart for me—and for my baby. Perhaps it helps her in her healing to write and express herself through poetry in the year that I marry. Perhaps she does not feel the need to give it to

107

me. The poem may be written as a gift to God who brings healing to her and to us.

In all the years that follow until her death, my Mother never gives me this tender poem that I would love receiving with all my heart. I never knew she ever wrote a poem! Yet here it is scribbled on a torn scrap of paper like she gives me with items on she wants me to get at the corner grocery store in writing I can never understand as a child. I hand the lists to Mr. Weyter, the grocer, to decipher on each visit.

I cry too, just contemplating that I might never have discovered it at all, yet I cry also because I do discover it. To see the title and the poem is like receiving a touch from Heaven. What if I had never discovered it? I am so grateful I do. I feel certain she never shows the poem to my Dad, but somehow I feel his presence in it, his influence. This is why I include it here, fully knowing that now in a new dimension he is aware of it. It also is a symbol of mysteries surrounding my Mother that my Dad lives with all of his married life of forty-nine years. I believe that day that from "somewhere over the rainbow" my very colorful Mother, for her name consists of two colors, Violet Gray, leaves me a gift more priceless than the pot of gold. My love for her too reaches to beyond the stars and she knows this.

The poem is titled Janice Elizabeth and appears in another book of mine. Perhaps it is significant to include here, for it is a most precious "find" in an old blue dishpan.

My Mother and Dad
(Violet and Ellis)

JANICE ELIZABETH

My lucky star—this little girl
    So peaceful in her bed,
With big blue eyes and curly hair
    And dimpled cheeks so red.

She grasped my little finger
    With her tiny slender hand
And held it tight in greeting
    Long ... that I would understand.

Her names are Janice and Elizabeth
    And echo in my heart
Of golden promise,
    That we'll never be apart.

And so I think in years to come
    That she will always be—
As on the day that she arrived
    My lucky star to me.

And now my Daughter's tiny tot
    My little June Leslie who—
Just like her Mother long ago
    Now holds my finger too.

—Mother
Written by Violet McKay Gray

It is significant also that I refer to my precious Rochester as "My Star"—one of numerous poems written for him in reference to this. This was written shortly after he passed and only appears in my book *Corridors*.

EVER WITH ME

Four months have fled.
   You softly tred
Into my days.
   I feel the rays
My Star so dear.
   I know you're here.

I pick up pen
   Begin to write
And that is when
   You send your light—
And poems flow
   Through heart and head.
I daily know
   You are not dead.

Ever with me
   Angel muse.
Forever sending
   Your dear clues.
That though you're gone—
   Invisibly—
With every dawn
   You walk with me.

For my Angel and Star   Jan
Rochester   July 28, 2002

Obstacles cannot crush me,
every obstacle yields to stern resolves.
He who is fixed to a star
does not change his mind.

        —Leonardo DaVinci

MEDITATION THIRTY-TWO

Heartsongs

I have a song, deep in my heart,
And only I can hear it.

—Mattie J.T. Stepanek, *Heartsongs*

When I am a child I do not remember walking around the house singing or doing so when involved in my play as many children do. It is possible I sing little lullabies to my dollies and stuffed animals that I love so much but at this point in time I have no recollection of this or many other things in my childhood. My Mother does not sing either as she cooks or works about the house as I remember, but she does sing often when she sits at the piano to play hymns or popular songs of the time from sheet music she frequently buys at Zaph's Music Store on Fifth Street in the business section of our community of Olney. Maybe my Mother is not allowed to take piano lessons when she is a girl since she has eight brothers and sisters and is the youngest child. I do not ask her about all of this because I never like to talk about the piano unless she forces me to speak of it. I never just start talking about anything to do with the piano even though I would like to know about Mother. Maybe she wants to be a well-known piano player when she grows up, even a concert pianist. Maybe I do not practice hard enough as she would practice when she is my age. She knows how to play the piano nicely, but she cannot play the classical music I have to learn. She plays the fun things—like the most popular songs and the hymns we sing at the Methodist Church. That is why I know a lot of the popular songs too, because she always buys the sheet music and plays them. But I have to practice only things like *Fur di Leise* and *Clair de Lune* (I hate them) and other similar pieces—and scales and all sorts of exercises. Every piece I have to memorize too. I cannot have another piece of music until I can play the one I am memorizing without any mistakes. When she is not around I sometimes play some of the popular songs I like, and I can play them fairly well though I am never taught them. Once Mother catches me and tells me it sounds terrible and to concentrate on my own music. One song she likes to play is Marie Elena. It is a very old song from when she is a young girl and she plays it so nicely. I can play it too, but she does not know it. Mother makes me practice an hour a day and I cannot go out side to play until I do. If she does not like my practicing she gets angry at me and I cannot go out that day, be it in Fall or Winter or Spring when I can be outdoors in the period after practicing and before dinner. But in summer when school is out, often I must stay inside if I do not practice well according to Mother's thinking and lose an entire day of summer fun with my friends.

But these are unhappy things to speak of and I am sidetracked in what few clear memories I hold from speaking about my Daddy and me and singing, which is my original intention. Did I tell you before that my Daddy is a Methodist?

When I am a little girl I sit silently with my parents in our little Methodist Church. Even if I feel inclined (and I will not!) I never speak or sing out in the service above a whisper at the proper time to speak or sing. The possibility of me spontaneously singing out vigorously and heartily can perhaps ridiculously be compared to my performing solo in the present on a Broadway stage. It can never happen. Not even in my dreams! Even if I have the voice of an Angel—which I do not! All I write of myself in this regard I feel fairly certain can be written of my Dad. I never know his singing voice! Never can I hear it in church while growing up when sitting next to him though his lips are moving and following the words of the hymn. Never does he sing around the house or with any special songs that might suddenly come on the radio or television. Never do I hear him sing later on with or for any of my own children yet he is a precious Pop-Pop to them and does anything in the world to please them, amuse them, or help them. Perhaps he has an amazing and appealing strong voice but is too shy as I am to liberate it and allow anyone to hear it. Perhaps he is going to sing for me in Heaven.

Though all my family always sings out their songs and have since they were small with the exception of one who only more recently is able to free his, and each member has a fine voice, like my Dad I still sing in a whisper at church and not at all at home. Bob often teases me and repeats the old familiar joke—*"sing over by the window and I'll help you out."*

As a young Mother I sing gently soft lullabies to my babies in the quiet sacred moments spent together. And I feel certain my Dad does the same soft singing for me as a baby. I always sing inside myself now though and I love music! My Rochester too is silent, but oh I know he too always sings inside himself while on earth and too, is singing in Heaven. Rochester and I sing duets all day long in our glorious silence while he is on earth next to me as I write at my desk and now too, in spirit.

And while my Dad does not sing, he enjoys whistling and to hear him do this makes me happy. He is a good whistler. And I too like to whistle and can whistle very well when younger. I am glad. I cannot do it as well now but it still is like a little gift from my Dad. Like Andy and Opie in the old TV series, I can imagine my Dad and me walking along together on a country road whistling.

In my book *Solace of Solitude* I write;

A grackle came again today many times sounding his song from the deck and table with his crackly voice—but it is wonderful and he believes he is singing a beautiful song. I stop to listen. He has seen me watching through the window and maybe he is even serenading me. I do appreciate him.

I go on to say that the grackle is teaching me and perhaps you a gentle lesson, for all my life I stifle my voice and the songs within me. (And in all the years of my Dad's life that I know and love him, he too stifles his voice.) I write:

Do not be ashamed of your song within. God put it there for you to dis-cover and sing aloud and its mysterious affect upon you will cause you to see life in a new way. Be like the grackle who serenades in a crackly voice but hears only his lovely song. And because of his confidence and spontaneity, I too hear only beauteous notes pouring out of his shiny brown feathered body.

Burghild Nina Holzer writes in her book on journal keeping. *A Walk Between Heaven and Earth encouraging words to my soul*—

Maybe my throat wants to tell me of all the songs held back. Held back in fear, or in doubt, or in anger, all the songs that the heart already knows that I have not voiced. Perhaps I need to walk in that place, down my throat to the vocal chords.

I identify with her deep feelings and words as if she is writing about myself, and lack of singing. I believe my Dad does also. She continues by writing that perhaps there is a big boulder she needs to discover sitting in her throat. Perhaps huge masses of words are compacted into stone. She considers that they can be words too frightening to face, words that have been pushed back or perhaps words too beautiful and tender to bring forth and admit. She closes her reflection by saying "*So many words waiting to be born, all held back.*"

I believe because of the problems and strangeness in our home that my Mother's sometimes weeks of silence cause, that my Dad and I are not liberated spiritually to sing aloud. We are bound and inhibited, like treading on glass and hoping not to crack what peace is existing at certain times.

We each have a song to sing in our hearts and yet so often we are silenced and our song dies and we are afraid to sing. Perhaps this is why I write so much as a young child. In the silence forced upon me and my Dad, I can still express myself in writing. I feel I have a voice. I believe my Dad's songs are given birth these past thirty years that he is in Heaven, and that Rochester too has an audible precious voice that speaks of the song in his heart. I hear his heartsong when he is here with me continuously. I hear his heartsong still in my dreams and prayers. Perhaps too, one day my songs will be born and we three will walk side by side singing along the byways and woodland paths of Heaven.

Everyone in the whole wide world
Has a special Heartsong.

—Mattie J.T. Stepanek, *Heartsongs*

This morning as I finish this meditation we hear a beautiful chirping and song. It is the lovely Red Winged Blackbird returning to Higher Ground. His song is emphasizing all I have written here.

When the birds are teaching me I hear Him.

—Brother Patrick Francis

MEDITATION THIRTY-THREE

Revisiting

In writing this book it causes me to reflect upon the last time I visited my parents' and uncle's graves. In my constant reading, studying, reflecting and praying during these past five years I now hold different truths concerning death, while still retaining my basic and strong Christian faith. These truths had entered my heart and soul following the passing of Rochester in March 2002 and before visiting the graves in December of that same year.

It seems right to share now this meditation written following that December visit that is a part of my book *Solace of Solitude*, the second book in my trilogy.

Things Remembered

> *Stranger call this not a place*
> *Of fear and gloom.*
> *To me it is a pleasant spot*
> *It is my husband's tomb.*

—Charles L. Wallis
(for my Mother, Dad, Uncle and a little unknown girl)

DECEMBER 3, 2002

Today is a significant day to me. We have been in Pennsylvania six days and will leave to drive home to New Hampshire tomorrow. It is only the second time I have gone back to our former hometown of Jenkintown since we moved to New Hampshire in January 1996. We are staying in the home of our daughter Barbara and her husband Francis, and their handsome and lovable cat Buddy. On this day of December third the

116

four of us go out on errands and on the way we drive into the Forest Hills Cemetery where my parents and uncle, all of whom I lost in a period of thirteen months from August 1977 to September 1978, are buried, along with a younger child who is sister to my Mother and Uncle. This is a cemetery I visited regularly alone from 1977 until moving to New Hampshire nineteen years later. Often I headed there deliberately or when out on errands, and would drive there to pray and tell my family members things on my heart or to sit and stare and cry. Their graves are all in a square plot together toward the back of the cemetery and a lovely small road is next to them. I could drive up and park and sit in the car by the graves to pray, or get out and stand there and talk and pray. I am thankful I took pictures of their headstones to have here in New Hampshire. Usually I sat in the car with the window rolled down. Often I was sad and sharing my problems with them. This was all comforting and I often wrote things down in a small journal while visiting. It was as if two worlds existed; my real one to which I would return to after the visits, and the one filled with mystery on the secluded hill in the cemetery.

Today I visit my Mother, Dad and Uncle's graves after a seven year absence, and too the little girl buried there in the fourth plot I never knew. Once back at our daughter's home I see myself again on the hill and imagine (as I did when I visited in person) not only my loved ones but also the dark gray suit my Uncle has on, and the dark blue of my Dad's, the pretty soft silky dress of shades of black and gray my Mother wears. She selected that new to wear to my Dad's and Uncle's Methodist services in 1977 and it seemed right to us to have her wear it for her own, and for her treasured heavenly meeting with the two she grieved for and longed to be with.

All of these things are remembered especially today on my Mother's birthday, but too again and again and again. I am learning to experience them in new ways in my new life.

> *He went before she did.*
> *She thought she would break,*
> *She felt she was fallin' apart.*
> *But still she remembers*
> *The last words he said*
> *As he held her hand close to his heart.*

—Willy Welch

She can help you more where she now is than she could have done on earth.

—C. S. Lewis
In a letter to a friend on the death of his wife.

A New Form of Visit from Dad

In this form of prayer one sits as in meditation and gradually becomes aware of the images that appear on the inner eye.

—Jan, *Beneath the Stars and Trees*

I do not believe I have ever seen my Dad before 2005 in a hypnogogic image. I see Rochester repeatedly in hypnogogic imagery since his passing, but not Dad. Even my dreams and visions of him have been few. But on February 4, 2005 I see my Dad late at night in hypnogogic imaging and I am so moved by it I do not want it to end.

My Dad is in a chair that resembles the one he sits in through the years by the front window at 6231. I see the imagery at a distance and he leans forward slightly and turns his head and looks directly at me. At first because the image is at a distance and it is dim, I think it is me. It looks slightly like my face and I can not see the detail of any clothing.

Then the image comes closer and it is my Dad! It may be the only time that I see him in this way. In my journal that day I write *"Why do I not see him more? Why?"*

I open a book of mine read twice in the past months, *The Afterlife Connection* by Dr. Jane Greer, a book that is a source of confirmations and help in my own afterlife connections, the day after I see my Dad in hypnogogic imagery. In the pages I find a *"find."* I tuck many significant scraps of paper, pictures and markers into my books while reading after Rochester passes, and this day in the pages is an unusual picture I forget I put there of my Dad. He is in his bedroom and there is a ragged circle around him. It is a print my daughter Barbara gives me a long time ago in a very small blue denim frame. The original picture is folded and creased all around the four sides to be made to fit into the small frame. When taken out it is unusual to see as I discover months before when I do just that. Bob makes me then enlarged 4x6 prints of it and it becomes even more other-worldly. My Dad is centered in the middle of this ragged circle as if in another dimension with small lines and cracks in the background. I am so fond of this picture seemingly from *"beyond"* to me, like a visit from him from *afar* each time I see it.

Bob tells me after reading this that that is the planet I am from— *"Afar."* In his unyielding perfect thinking he truly believes me to be *"far out."* You can imagine what our discussions are like. Meanwhile the small version of the picture hidden with the ethereal circle sits on my desk in the blue denim frame. Only the ends of Dad's own bureau and night table can be seen in the enlargement to tell me where he is in the picture. It is important to pay attention to pictures I learn after Rochester passes, for we often discover mysteries in them and what before goes unnoticed may now appear as a hidden image, be it person or persons or objects or animals. I write about this in a more complete way in journals and in a previous book.

To suddenly now see my Dad there in this picture tucked in a book with a title regarding *"afterlife"* the day after I see him in hypnogogic imagery is surely to me a *"sign"* he is here with me in spirit. I pray repeatedly he be in more contact and too, I wear his large ring on my left thumb.

I would like to be able to take a photo of a dream.

—Helene Cixous

and I would add—and also of a hypnogogic image.

Ellis (Dad), year unknown. Picture had been folded into a little frame, giving an unusual appearance (other-worldly).

MEDITATION THIRTY-FIVE

Contemplating the Cemetery

*I had gone to the cemetery. I do not believe that Jason is any more
in his grave than he is in Tahiti, but I relish the serenity of sitting
by "his rock" and the unlikely chance of anyone stopping by
to talk about the weather.*

—Sandy Goodman, Love Never Dies—
A Mother's Journey From Loss to Love

Up until January 1996 when we moved permanently to New Hampshire, the above words of the author could be mine also. It is now four years and six months since I last visited that cemetery and those blessed graves back in Pennsylvania, for we have not returned there since that time.

I have learned through my reading that many aside from myself find it consoling to visit and spend time alone at a loved one's grave. It is not at all morbid as some may believe. For me it was deeply consoling even though I know my loved ones are in Heaven. It was a place of refuge for me during times in my life that were extremely difficult and when I no longer had my parents or uncle physically with me to confide in or receive comfort or support. And since that time of my last visit I have continuously read books on grieving and afterlife to the exclusion of all else for I am being led in ways that I do not ever contradict. I know I am on a guided path. It is during this period and not long after this grave side visit of December 3, 2002 to my parents and uncle that I read the author's book whose words open this meditation, and read it numerous times more in these past years. I do not usually read books only once, or it is rare that I do, if it is book that overwhelms and feeds my soul and enters my life like a friend sent by God.

I did not know until 2002 that it was not strange I should want to spend those times of quiet retreat in that cemetery. I did not know it was truly acceptable. I felt strange yet needed the peace I found there from my heartaches and from missing those loved ones. It was Rochester entering Heaven and my reading and searching that followed, that allowed me to know it was a consoling and healing thing to do. Many authors I have read would tell you so, not just the lovely author I have quoted. We learn so many truths and mysteries are revealed when the passing of a precious loved one takes place. To not speak of our loved ones again or have tears is wrong. As I have written elsewhere I was scolded more than once when I cried for my parents by another older family member. I was liberated spiritually through Rochester and his passing to grieve anew for my family members and to grieve deeply, deeply for him, my beloved Chester. The visit to the graves of those loved ones several months after Rochester's passing began a new relationship with those loved ones causing them to be present in spirit so much more than in the past.

Though there is still not the freedom to speak about family members in Heaven to other family here on earth except to Bob, or about Rochester, I am spiritually content and fulfilled in the amazing connections that have been given to me. They are constant and ever comforting and surprising and enduring. I am eternally grateful.

> *When I went to sit by Jason's Rock, I often blew bubbles, sending them off with reflections of love. It became a ritual, and a bottle of bubbles sits at Jason's gravesite year round.*
>
> —Sandy Goodman

What a wonderful, comforting ritual of love. If I should return to those graves in Pennsylvania I too will send up bubbles, but I have already done it numerous times here by the lake, for I do not need to be standing by their graves. I know Rochester enjoys them too, *precious reflections of love* that hold new significance for me.

An old song published in 1919 often sung and one my Mother played on the piano was—

I'm forever blowing bubbles
Pretty bubbles in the air—
They fly so high
Nearly reach the sky—
Then like my dreams,
They fade and die.

MEDITATION THIRTY-SIX

Images

Life is not measured by the number of breaths we take,
but by the moments that take our breath away.

—Unknown

In my book *Solace of Solitude—Afterlife Visits*, I write that on June 2, 2003, my Dad's birthday, Rochester makes himself present in still yet another dimension, that of Hypnogogic Imagery. I see Rochester clearly in this way numerous times, yet before he goes to Heaven I never see anyone I ever know personally in Hypnogogic Imagery. But I do see many people, all of whom are strangers. As I write in a previous book, I see many clear and amazing scenes and people that I describe in this unusual dimension but never before anyone I ever knew. But this all changes when Rochester passes, for then he begins to appear to me in the visual form and does to this day. It is both startling and utterly consoling and I am so grateful. It is quite possible that all I receive in these visions before his passing is in preparation for me to have the awareness of this other world and dimension so I might be totally prepared for the gift of Rochester to come through and appear.

On this particular night on my Dad's birthday when in bed in the dark and before sleep as I pray, I see Chester up close. Just his precious face is so very close to mine, his big golden eyes looking into our one soul. It is so in detail and beautiful exactly as in real life, and all the while his heat and electricity generate on my legs as they do before his handsome countenance appears. It is such a gift—and I feel it might be such from both Rochester and my Dad, a divine gift on my Dad's birthday.

Other gifts of Hynogogic imagery with Rochester are given frequently in the years since then. In the wee hours of morning, almost 3 AM on March 27, 2007, and after prayers and praying to see Rochester, two images of his sweet face come to me. One is a front view and very close. In the other Chester is looking more to the side yet I can see both of his eyes. His left side of his face is to me. In both images his eyes are golden and so very beautiful as always. In the first image he looks straight into me in such love. The images make me cry. He is so handsome and I feel his presence and love. I am in another fragment of time as if washed in light yet physically in a darkened room.

Often in prayer I have to wait for images to appear and some never do. But on these nights in 2003 and 2007, as soon as I close my eyes my beloved little Rochester appears an inch or so from my face while I am half sitting, half lying in the dark. How often in real life he comes up close to me like that to bump his little head into mine numerous times while his paws are on my shoulders. And then we settle down to sleep as he lies on my legs facing me, his little paws in my hand.

I want to share many of these experiences that come to me since he passes but now I tell you of these two only that are four years apart.

It is as important to them to communicate with us as it is to hear from them. Your pets know how much they mean to you, and they are still with you. Your pets will be waiting for a happy reunion when you cross over.

—George Anderson, *Walking in the Garden of Souls*

Rochester

Before settling down for prayer and sleep upon my legs, Rochester often climbed gently up the front of me as I sat in a half-reclining position and he would push his little forehead against mine numerous times, a form of kiss. Often he would gently pat my cheek with his soft white marshmallow paw, a tender touch of his love—not only at night but often in our writing room when he was on my lap or desk. Thus this poem was written for him on his birthday May 30, 1995 with great love and in gratitude.

SOUL'S TOKEN

My kitten's tender paw, thou soft, small treasure*
Upon my cheek or hand—brings joy unspeakable, and pleasure
That cannot be written—nor spoken.
It is his giving of love, his token
From his soul—expressed in merest touch.
And I receive—and love him, oh so very much.

*quote by Heinrich Heine (German poet)

The Questionable Keepsake

Here in our very small cottage, the back left area just outside the bathroom has a wall between that bathroom door and the kitchen. To me what is placed upon the wall is very attractive, meaningful and memory filled. The lower half of the wall has a three shelf maple bookcase in front of it that has been in all of our homes since we married. Before that the bookcase was Bob's. The bookcase is filled with many wholistic source books and books vegetarian in subject including cook books. Also there are many books on nature and animals and a large copy of Henry David Thoreau's *Walden*. Above this bookcase hanging on the wall are two large wooden shadow boxes each with forty-four compartments of various sizes one above the other and rather look like one large shadowbox. Beneath these are two smaller wooden shadowboxes. The compartments of all four are filled with sentimental objects and treasures that were given to me as gifts through the years or that I found significant enough to add to the collection myself. A number of things were my Mother's. There are many animal figures. They are in the majority. Religious figures and Angels also are represented and several rocks. There is a hand-carved wooden Indian head carved by George and Bob when George was a Boy Scout and it is a handsome carving. The two larger shadow boxes are identical. When I first saw them in a country store in New Hampshire in the early 80s and they were so inexpensively priced yet wonderfully crafted, I bought two. One was for our home in Jenkintown and one for our cottage here in New Hampshire. I had always wanted a shadow box and had never had one so I doubled up. When we began to spend more time in New Hampshire before moving here permanently I brought the Pennsylvania shadow box back home to its state of origin and we combined them on this small wall.

The keepsakes seem different. I easily detect which is the New Hampshire shadow box for in that one there are numerous specific treasures to me all from my childhood and teen years. These specific ones are all connected to my Dad. One is disturbing yet I must always keep it there. In one little compartment is a white Scotty dog that is a pin. It is trimmed in black and across the body is the name *Janice*. I was with both my Dad and Mother when this pin was bought for me. It was a period where people were displaying their names on decorative things but that is occurring even in the present as well. I used to enjoy wearing it as a young girl. Also there is a wooden pin of an elephant made by my Dad when I was very young. He worked on such a project of that sort and other wooden pins and objects as a request from my Mother for a group that she was a member of and who used them to raise money for a worthy cause I no longer remember. I was a child.

Too, there is a china figurine of an elf dressed in green sitting cross-legged. I have always been entranced by fairies and elves and gnomes which is obvious if one sees my gardens here, and the lawn figurines within them. Many small animals too in the shadow box are from these earlier years, animals of all sorts in china along with animals I bought

all through my life or were given; wild animals particularly deer and moose and sweet cats, dogs and rabbits and others. All of these items from my girlhood were bought in stores on the boardwalk of Ocean City, New Jersey when we

Picture of my Dad's cigarette light (in upper right-hand corner of shadow box) with keepsakes.

were happily vacationing there by the sea in summers past. My Dad was with me for the purchase of the Scotty dog pin and the green elf and too, numerous little animals, so they hold sentimental significance. My Mother also was there at times. But the other item that is in the shadow box that belonged to my Dad and is not a gift is the disturbing one.

It is a silver cigarette lighter rectangular in shape about two inches high. It has a small round blue Masonic seal on the front. It was given to him as a gift years and years ago. On the back are his initials vertically placed in the lower right corner engraved very nicely. Like the tie clasp he wore that I teased him about, this lighter has EGG on it too. This lighter is nice to look at but represents to me his struggle with smoking and his frequent sadness and annoyance of himself over not being able to stop smoking forever, and then his eventual horrific loss of his larynx. It is a many faceted symbol to me, this lighter, not at all pleasing, but because it was his and his hands once held it, I will forever keep it in my shadow box. Obviously it entered his life during the same period as his Masonic ring that I wear. Though he stopped wearing the ring eventually he continued to use the lighter. I cannot say for how long for he also used regular matches as well.

Perhaps to write of this is not important now, but anything that he bought for me or gave to me or was his is important and thus I am feeling the need to record it on paper now. The lighter I claimed for myself after my Mother passed away and I found it in one of my Dad's bureau drawers.

Another author that I have mentioned elsewhere in this book and have come to know recently as if a friend in spirit writes:

I only knew that since my father could die at any time, I had to save every bit of concrete proof that I was loved before he vanished from the earth. The things he gave me were my certificates of love, my diplomas, my credibility.

—Geneen Roth

She too had had a difficult childhood. And as I did continually when Rochester was with me in body, she saved tufts of her sweet cat Blanche's fur after brushing him nightly and thousands of photographs she took of him.

These were only two similarities of our eccentricities of love. She claims this classifies her for a new definition of insanity aside from the keepsakes connected to her father. If this be so, then I too lay claim to insanity, but I have realized that all along about myself. I believe there are "many of us" out there that love so, so deeply like this be it a sweet father or a beloved cat or mate or friend or any other.

And since I cannot write about my father's lighter from "holier than thou" height, I must make a confession or I would be doing my Dad an injustice in my estimation in only sharing about his addiction that he could not give up until he was forced to by surgery. I confess that I too smoked and truly am not proud of it. Whether I would have if my Dad had not, I cannot honestly say. But because his pack was always evident by his chair in the sunparlor near the front window, I eventually succumbed and tried one of his Camels since some of my teenage friends were already smoking. I am not proud of this either, and felt like a bad person each time I did. Add to that fact that I used his cigarettes made my guilt deeper. In time I could occasionally afford a pack on my small allowance but only bought Camels which were rather considered a man's cigarette and stronger. But I was afraid if I left evidence in our home, I would be caught if it was not a Camel. Time passed and I was eventually caught by my Mother, but despite a developing, persistent cough I continued, now addicted. Bob too had begun to smoke before I knew him in Dental School. Before we married we agreed that we would stop smoking once we did marry. And we did stop! We had only one pack of Camels and following our wedding and on our flight to San Diego that same weekend (for Bob had to be back on duty) we agreed during a layover in Denver Airport that we would stop promptly. We agreed we could smoke the cigarettes in this pack and when they were gone we were done smoking forever. They were rapidly diminished soon after even though butts were saved as a last desperate resource. I write in complete honesty that when that pack was gone we never smoked again. Ever! I do not say it was easy, but we did it "cold turkey" and kept our promise to this very day. And God must have been leading us for we were married in early January and I learned in February that I was expecting baby June. Nine months later in October she was born. How terrible it would have been had I smoked unknowingly while pregnant. I only wish my Dad had stopped then too. I would have had his loving presence for years and years longer because he was a healthy man. He might even be with me still today at 102. Many people live longer lives now, long past 100. I like to think he would still be here instead of his passing at seventy-three as he did. Though smoking did not kill him, it depleted him and he was never the same man of stamina in the six months after his larynx removal and preceding his sudden death from another cause. All these years there is the great possibility I could have been blessed by his fun and humor and love, and all of our nineteen grandchildren who never met him could know their wonderful great grandfather.

To All Smokers

Ash Wednesday—how odd
On a day with this name
Associated with God—
Dad should lose the game!

His cigarettes—each day
Created ashes—
He had smoked all the way—
Now—back lashes!

He would tell you in deep remorse—
To reverse your course.

For my Dad   Jan
Ellis George Gray   February 23, 1994
—with love—
Died August 21, 1977

This poem speaks of the day his larynx was removed.

MEDITATION THIRTY-EIGHT

Grieving Through Writing and Reading

I scour libraries and bookstores for guidance; I find many different kinds of books about death and loss, but none of them speaks to the raw primal terror I am experiencing. No one seems as desperate or wild as me.

—Geneen Roth, *The Craggy Hole in My Heart and The Cat Who Fixed It*

I do not read books on grieving when my Dad dies. It does not enter my mind nor does anyone else mention books or give me a book as a gift to help me. I know my Mother receives no books. This is strange considering books are a huge part of my life ever since I am a little girl though this is not so with my Mother. Small devotional books are on her bureau and bedside table, but I never see her sit and read as my Dad and I do. Perhaps it is something she does at times when I am not aware.

And so, I do not read books on grieving when my Dad dies. I help my Mother by writing all her notes in regard to my Dad's passing in response to the enormous amount of notes, letters and flowers she receives. My Mother is cared about and well known by many who are customers at her costume jewelry store in downtown Philadelphia and too, through her attendance and work at her Methodist Church. Many are writing to her because they are fond of my Dad, yet some write who do not know him but know my Mother who is suffering a deep loss. And indeed she is suffering a deep loss. It is not that she is not capable of replying to the many, many notes and letters, but she is truly heartbroken and she asks if I will do this. It is a work of love to write again and again of my Dad and to respond to these kindnesses. It takes many weeks to do this along with regular living and caring for my own family and replying to my own personal cards and letters I receive in regard to my Dad's passing, but I am so pleased she asks me to do this writing. Along with all of this writing I am also pouring myself out in a journal. And when my dear Uncle passes away in November three months after my Dad, my Mother's only living brother and relative, I do the same in his regard. This is my Uncle Elmer that I love since I am a tiny girl and who I write about later in several of my books, and who is a part of my life and our childrens's lives. This is the dear Uncle who sends me as a teenager to art school in Philadelphia. I reply to the many letters my Mother receives of sympathy.

By now she is so depleted in grief we even talk her into coming to New Hampshire with us over Thanksgiving to our cottage she has never seen. Here we try to help her in many gentle ways. She carries pictures of my Dad and Uncle with her in a little plastic folder that I now own and that she shows to our girls and George. I understand now more than ever in these present years the importance of photos of dear loved ones who are now In Heaven. I carry two with me always of Rochester back to back plasticized. They are a comfort beyond words.

When my Mother too passes away from a broken heart in September of the next year in 1978, I do the same appreciative writing in response to all the sympathy cards and notes and letters, for this time they are for me, and for my family also. There are so, so many! I have them still in a lovely container. And too, I continue to write in my journal. All of this writing is my therapy. I see that now.

> *(I am—yet what I am, none cares or knows:*
> *My friends forsake me like a memory lost —)*
>
> —John Clare

I still do not read books on grieving. Instead it is then the period and slightly before that I begin reading books about my Protestant church history to learn more of this and the books about the saints. This leads to books by other Church Fathers and especially to the discovery of Trappist Monk Thomas Merton and his many writings that speak to me so directly and uniquely. All of this is my spiritual help then and deep prayer and leads to my entering the Catholic Church three months after my Mother's passing. No, I still do not read books on grieving. It never enters my mind to do so, nor do I receive any spiritual help from anyone nor does anyone in my family speak to me in any depth about my three loved ones. I am on my own in this new country of the soul and it is a strange place to me. Death is ignored after a very short short period.

> *Even the dearest that I love the best*
> *Are strange—nay, rather, stranger than the rest.*
>
> —John Clare

I write in my previous book *Solace*, how I am even reprimanded with the words "stop crying" on two occasions by an older relative for my spontaneous tears that flow at the thought and mention of my Dad. There is always someone who wishes to change or squelch you, or hush you, or diminish you because they themselves fear death and do not want it in the present moment. They wish to hurry through it and hurry everyone else too. An author, Sandy Goodman, who is a friend to me in spirit along this corridor and to whose book, *Love Never Dies,* I return to often, writes:

> *Friends and family members want us to move on, get over it, find closure.—I did the only thing I felt capable of doing. I pretended to be "progressing" through the grief normally.*

Grief does not get better, it gets different. That is said by someone else beside myself whom I trust. Each individual is different. There is no handbook for grief.

For many like myself, there is acceptance but not closure. Closure is an inappropriate and unacceptable term for those like myself, and has become almost a "catch phrase."

If you deeply love you never get over the death of a loved one, but you gently move through it. This too, is said by someone wiser than I and not only by myself alone. Grief never goes away but it changes with time. It is always with you if your love is deep and is a precious gift to carry within. Everywhere we go we carry our loved ones and grief.

If the dead be truly dead, why should they still be walking in my heart?
—Winneap Shosone, Medicine Man

In my book *Solace of Solitude* I write these words:

There are so many in the world living with grief for it is a part of them they never wish to release until they are reunited with their beloved loved one in Heaven. It is their gift in a sense, their privilege to carry another they loved so deeply in their own being, in their heart. But human beings basically are uncomfortable with sadness and grief and many feel awkward and inadequate in the presence of one who carries grief. And too, many discredit them and think something is terribly wrong with the individual. There is. They are experiencing a "new landscape of the soul" where grief abides and remains and is carried in deepest love and privilege. And it is there they dwell even while in the world and life goes on.

I write those words in my second book following the passing of Rochester. Grief is ever fresh. By then, however, I turn to books and do so by Monday, March 18, 2002 as I write in my first book *Corridors*, my journal following Rochester's entrance into Heaven on March 8th. I need books on grieving desperately! I know in my heart I need this specific help. Writing all the responses to the letters of condolences for my parents and uncle and writing in my journal and reading spiritual books carries me through the aftermath of their passings while not being able to discuss it all in depth for lack of listeners. But I know immediately I need this new help of special books on grieving when I see history repeating itself. I am consumed by grief. Bob is supportive and kind, but lets me "be."

A quotation from one of these books I have read multiple times and will continue to read interspersed with my other reading, is one I relate to deeply as I do to the entire book and all books by this author. These lines are just a portion of it.

Sometimes no one will want to hear what you're going through. You are going to have to learn to carry a great burden and most of your learning will be done alone.

—Ron Kovic, *Born on the Fourth of July*
from the *Lessons of Love* by Melody Beattie

Grieving people that lost loved ones on the plane that crashed in the water off New York in January 2007 said that other people avoided them, did not talk to them. They felt isolated in their grief. This describes how I was and am with Rochester and in regard to my Dad, Mother and other family members, isolated. Rarely did anyone talk of them—rarely speak of them. Precious beings. Nor is my father-in-law's passing mentioned.

I refer you now to the quotation at the beginning of this meditation by Geneen Roth, for it speaks so deeply to me of those earlier days and it is as if I write it myself. I cannot emphasize the importance of books. It is why I also began writing my Trilogy in regard to grief and about the travelling along that *Corridor*. No one wants me to speak of Rochester and he is so priceless to me I cannot bear indifference and it adds to my grieving. I need to read about grief because I am submerged in it. I need to read about grief in regard to losing a beloved companion and the books I choose regarding human loss are appropriate for my grief regarding Rochester. When you love, grief is grief. I buy four books on grieving and a journal that first day I go to Waldens Book Store in Rochester, in the town where I adopt Rochester in 1986. Now five years later I am still buying books on grief and afterlife and the hereafter for it is how God and Rochester are leading me to help myself and others. I live in the now. Another woman also writes of the necessity of reading saying:

> *My father died so suddenly. It was such a shock. Ever since then, I've wanted to know where he is. I would go to Borders and get stacks of books about peoples' experiences. I would read them straight through in one night. I didn't know who wrote them. I was obsessed.*

> —John Edward from *Crossing Over*

The new journal I find March 18th, 2002 is so perfect. The night sky here in New Hampshire is always so brilliant with stars and the moon in all its forms, and it is a magical and spiritual part of living here. It is part of my life with Chester and always shall be. I write and still write poems for him comparing him to the stars and angels. He is both of these in my life forever.

The new journal has two half moons facing each other and touching at their points forming a whole, which speaks of an eternal circle to me and Rochester's and my forever and unbroken circle of love. The journal is even titled *"Forever"* above the moon, and the sky is deep shades of night blue and red.

Arriving home is the hardest moment of all, for always after we open the door he runs briefly onto the enclosed porch to greet us, then dashes into the bedroom to await me. I go directly there and we sit on the side of the bed together while he too walks on my lap and rolls around next to me wanting to be patted, and bumping his sweet head into mine. I let our little ceremony of welcome continue until he ends it. I go into the bedroom too on this day of buying books and journal upon arriving home. I go into the bedroom every night or day since his passing upon arriving home for that same little ritual now in spirit.

There is no difference in grieving be it for a beloved animal or human. I share anew words that I included in a previous book but are so precious as to be included again. Author and renowned composer Martin Scot Kosins, whose music has been performed and recorded internationally, has written in his book, *Maya's First Rose—Diary of a Very Special Love*—

> *Most people have experienced the loss of a loved one. So they try, each in their own way, to make you feel they understand how sad you are.*
>
> *The world understands less the pain of losing an animal. This is because many people have never felt for themselves the true love of an animal. So you cannot really expect these people to realize that your love for a pet may be greater than your love for the dearest people in your life.*
>
> *The bond is different and can never be put into words. It is a bond that only The Heart understands.*

He also discloses—

> *A quiet thought entered my mind.*
> *"Maya, we're still together."*
> *Just then, she looked at me—*
> *and time stopped.*
> *What I felt could only be described as Peace. The kind of Peace I had read about in Ancient Books. A Peace which entered my heart and never left.*

And I remember thinking, "If a hand came down from Heaven, and lifted me off the earth—I could go quietly, peacefully and with no sorrow at all."

I can feel that same Peace again each time I think of Maya, and the joy we found in each other.

The Miracle has become a fact.

The above quotations, taken from *Maya's First Rose* touch my soul and bring tears with each reading of them through past years and to this present moment. They have also appeared in my book *A Pilgrim on Life's Road*. These words and Martin's entire book spoke to me again and again even before Rochester went to Heaven and I grieved for Marty and his precious dog Maya. Now in these past five plus years his book and Marty's kindnesses and spiritual friendship are a forever part of my journey. His words grace the covers of three of my previous three books, my Trilogy. In my heart I truly believe Maya and Rochester have met in Heaven, though each continue to be always at our sides.

That night of March 18, 2002 I begin reading my first new book on grieving. I say a prayer that this one, and the others, are supportive in ways I cannot quite yet understand, for I am only beginning to know this grief. It is almost like an entity. It is always there. Rochester is helping me too, then, and five years later. He is always my star and little teacher and angel.

AN ANGEL'S TOUCH

We hold hands when we're alone.
      This is only known
            by one or two—
                  but I will tell you
That it is the most moving thing,
      like the brush of an Angel's wing—
To feel that soft, small white paw—
      feather-light with no hint of claw
Resting on my hand.
      Only few can understand.

Then I place my other hand upon his paw—
      and it is the dearest phenomenon I ever saw—
For he then puts his other paw on me—
      (and I do not want to be free!)
And our little stack of love and affection
      at times brings tears—and reflection—
Upon our life together and moments captured
      for we two so alike—become enraptured
By the simplest things,
      —as paws brushing hands like Angels' wings.

Dedicated to   Jan
Rochester   August 28, 1996
with great love
for the anniversary of the
day of his adoption—(and mine)
June 23, 1986

Rochester

MEDITATION THIRTY-NINE

His Visit to Sanbornville

It is a warm night in August. We drive out of our woods in early evening and down Route 153 heading for Sanbornville, fifteen minutes away. Since we prefer life in the woods to any social events, this is a rare occasion. A "big band" concert has been advertised and this is music of nostalgia from our younger teen years. Two years earlier we attended a similar concert in a huge barn at the top of the hill above Sanbornville and because it is enjoyable we decide to attend the concert tonight. It is being held in the Town Hall at the base of the hill from where the barn and pastures are. The street and parking lot are filled with cars upon our arrival and after finding a space we park and enter the Town Hall. We are absorbed into the crowd of people ascending the stairs to the large meeting room on the second floor where the concert is being held. Rows of chairs are already quite filled and we wait just inside the door way to eye a possibility of two empty seats. Before any come into my view, a man walks by me close enough to brush my arm causing me to center on him instead. At the brief glance I have of him in profile I am stopped in my existence there as if by an invisible force. I am staring at my father, my Dad! Before I can have the experience completely register within my being, my Dad is sucked up into the throng heading for the back of the auditorium. I feel my eyes widen and my heart beat faster as I turn to tell Bob about whom I just saw as we too move with the crowd. Bob listens but does not speak, just urging me by his expression to keep walking. He is probably thinking "oh no" within himself for he feels he lives in the real world and I in some alternate reality.

Silently we move down the aisle and around the back of the room and up the right, walking along side of the many rows of chairs on our left and rows of windows on our right. All the seats are taken until we suddenly spy two empty chairs on the end of a row about eight rows from the stage. We quickly and quietly slip into those. What good fortune! Now I am sitting for the concert between a stranger, and Bob who is on the end. The man on my left is talking to someone behind him and his back is to me. Minutes later an announcement is being made from the stage and the audience settles down to listen, and the man next to me turns and faces front. His moving causes me to glance at him, and I learn in that startling moment before I almost slip like water from my chair onto the floor, that I am looking at my Dad! Out of all the seats in this huge auditorium I am sitting in the one next to my Dad, the Dad who has been lost in the crowd only a short period ago. My heart is pounding and I immediately look to the front. I am too emotionally paralyzed to yet turn to my right and tell Bob. Too, I am crying. Finally I whisper to Bob over the announcements from the stage, that I am sitting next to my Dad. He smiles and leans slightly forward to see him, but with no comment. We settle back now as the band begins to play an old song of the past.

I use this opportunity to turn my head slightly and take in my father. My heart continues to pound as I look at his profile. That is all he is permitting but it is enough to wipe me out emotionally within. It is surely his profile, hair, glasses and gentle appearance. I am totally distracted by his presence. He has become the music for me, not the louder big band music from the platform.

I look down at his right arm. His white shirt is softly rolled up and a portion of his lower arm is exposed and so near me. It is his arm, my Dad's arm, and oh yes, it is his hand. How well I remember his hands. I just stare and stare at his hand and then steal another glance at his profile. I am sitting next to my Dad! What am I to do? Why am I not squealing or hugging him? He looks as he did in his last years with me. Only I have changed for it has been twenty eight years since I last saw that same right hand on the side rail of his bed in Germantown Hospital, and his finger raised to indicate his love and goodbye to me as we stood in the hall outside of his room. I stare ahead again to observe all that is taking place on the platform but not really in tune with it all. My Dad is sitting next to me on the left and I am caught and held in a long ago moment of time that has drifted into the present.

Except for my head that turns ever so slightly on occasion, I am a statue on a chair afraid my slightest movement might cause him to change or leave. Suddenly there is a solo by the drummer arising from the music and I center on him positioned on the left side of the band. He is excellent and I watch his hands perform before glancing at his face. What is happening?? Again I am blown away into the ether! The man playing the solo is my Dad! His face is his, his arms and body, and I am in disbelief! Again tears roll down my cheeks. My Dad is on the platform too!! In years past before I was born and maybe even shortly after, my Dad played drums in a band. That is all I know. But the evidence, his drumsticks, remained in a kitchen drawer during my growing up years. After his passing the drum sticks came into my possession. I had never heard him play, but now I am listening to him and looking at him. Oh he is good! He is really good!

After his solo he is somehow obscured by the men around him and his presence is lost to me. I am just weakened within by it all and look at Bob. He too is watching and I know he knows. He says nothing. Things like this are not his choice for discussions. Perhaps later.

I gently look to my left and my Dad is still there. Is he still there when my drummer dad is playing his solo? I am in such a God given twinkling of time I just silently give thanks that I am being given such gifts from the Afterlife. What is happening to me is not moot. I am being blessed and anointed and touched by a dimension in which my Dad and Rochester reside. Tonight my Dad and I sit next to each other at a concert after twenty-eight years of his physical absence, and then he plays a solo for me on his drums. He allows chairs to remain empty next to him that Bob and I might sit. He does not speak or turn to me. He allows me to take him into my eyes and mind and heart anew, helping me to remember what it was like to sit next to him, to see his profile and his shirt and hands. He does not wear a short sleeved shirt. He never did. He allows me his presence so overwhelmingly that it will forever be with me, a touch from beyond to hold me until I enter eternity and see him forever again.

I do not speak to him just as I do not run after my Dad in the checkout line years before when he visits me. I cannot speak to him or interrupt what I have been given. I do not believe it is my basic shyness. It is not out of fear. I believe I am believing I may intrude upon some great and Holy gift that is being sent, and to try to obtain more may upset a precious eternal plan. I am blessed, anointed, and will be forever grateful.

My Dad rises but does not turn full face to me. Instead he turns to his left and moves away from Bob and me following the other people on our row that are leaving. Bob and I momentarily remain in our seats. I follow my Dad with my eyes until once again he is lost in the crowd.

I came to know knowledge concerning the extraordinary gift I was given that evening, and too, years before in 1993 when I believe I saw my Dad then also in the check-out line immediately before me in the supermarket. I take notes on the subject from a man I have come to know and trust since Rochester's passing in 2002 through the many books he has written and his television programs and his honesty and integrity. And above all through his strong faith in God. John Edward states *that when you see someone and you instantly believe it is your loved one who has passed, as I saw my Dad, it is really your loved one placing their energy over or on the person. This is done by your loved one to bless you or to be near to you in that way.*—Amen.— This gift is called *Overlapping*.

> *Bemoan not the departed with excessive grief. The dead are devoted and faithful friends; they are ever associated with us.*
>
> —Confucius

*Dad (Ellis), some years after I married and left home,
sitting in his favorite corner of his sunparlor.*

MEDITATION FORTY

Dreams

It is in our dreams that many of us first experience
an ongoing relationship with a loved one who has died.

—Alexandra Kennedy from *Your Loved One*
Lives On Within You

Often we are unable to fully absorb and accept the death and impact upon us of someone we dearly love. If there was an attempt by others to silence you about your loved one's passing as there was in my life, as years pass you so welcome the constant love that remains and pervades your daily living knowing that that attempt to silence did not win. Some are so afraid of death themselves they cannot bear for anyone else to freely speak of death, or of their loved ones they too wish to express feelings for to others.

So when I have a dream of my Dad thirty years after his entering Heaven, I am so utterly grateful and overwhelmed. It is a new confirmation that he is ever with me. It is not that I have not had other dreams of him in the past, but that after a long span I just have a new one! And too, to be dreaming of him after thirty years of his physical absence tells me overwhelmingly he is ever present to me now and forever. Dreams are reassuring and often I have dreams of Rochester that are vivid and life-like and he is present as he was in life. These are visions I have recorded in journals and in my books. I feel if they are written of in my books they help others to not doubt the gift of presence of loved ones they receive in and through dreams and visions also. Books have always been a great strength and inspiration to me and especially those on grieving and afterlife since the passing of Rochester.

145

I did not have help like this after the passing of my parents and uncle. My special library I have created just of books on these subjects of afterlife and grieving and contacts by our loved ones in Heaven is now enormous. And though I add books to it continually I also regularly reread these treasured books multiple times; two, three, four and many have been read much more. But first I had to write my own book after Rochester passed. I had to write to help myself in my grief and so *In Corridors of Eternal Time* came to completion. Before it was published I had begun writing another book and then another—until a Trilogy on these subjects relating to both humans and animals (for there is no difference when we grieve for a loved one) was completed.

I did not discover books to read on grieving until after Rochester passed and I was writing my own book and did not discover books on afterlife until several months later. All these books I read also gave me new help and knowledge regarding all my loved ones who passed. As always Rochester had helped and guided me from Heaven just as he had always while sharing life on earth with me.

One of the first books I buy about Afterlife along with my books about grieving is a book by John Edward titled *One Last Time*. In the reading of it I am comforted and have things happening in my life through Rochester confirmed in the pages. But John speaks of dreams stating they are spirits' way of communicating with us directly. Not every dream of a dead relative is a visit. This is important to say. Many are our way of dealing with loss. But he goes on to say that we can distinguish between a dream that is a visit and a dream that is just a dream. He states *"A visit is profound, a gift. It feels incredibly vivid and real, and stays with us much longer than a standard dream."* This is so comforting to realize. Most dreams dissolve after a few hours from our memory unless we write them down as I try to do, but a visit will be clearly remembered for years and years.

Regard as evidence that you dreamed at a deeper level than your conscious mind could understand or hold if you wake up not remembering what you were taught or shown. Often your learning will turn up during the day regarding a deeper realization of faith, or a special kind of silence or feeling, or guidance or courage to act in a certain way or to follow your heart. I have made reference to similar thoughts elsewhere and too, profound insights by George Anderson in his book *Walking in the Garden of Souls*.

And so I have a dream of my Dad and it just means so very much. On the night of March 3, 2007 shortly after 2:30 AM, I dream of my Dad for the first time in what seems so long to me. We are in a room together and other people are in the room with us but they are walking away from us. I do not know who they are. My Dad and I just stand together facing each other. We stand to the left of these people walking away from us. My back is to myself as I view my vision of this as my Dad and I are talking. My Dad is somewhat half laughing and using his arms and hands to indicate what he is speaking of but I do not know what this is. It is not a usual way of my Dad's to use motions. I am so happy to see him and I watch as if from the sidelines. (I see the back of my head and shoulders in the dream.) Perhaps he visits me in this dream because I am writing this book about him. Perhaps his happy-like gestures to me are motions he is using to help express his words to me that I am unable to hear, words of approval about this book. I am hoping that. And I am thankful for this clear vision of my Dad looking well and healthy and the same way he appears in the years before his final year. He is talking in the dream but I do not know if his voice is silent or audible. But in Heaven I know it is audible for in Heaven we are healed and whole. In Heaven he again has his larynx.

Perhaps he is telling me that though others walked away either in actuality or figuratively when my loved ones passed away and no one would speak of these passings, or barely so, including Rochester's, he has always been with me.

I thank him for this wonderful appearance into my life each night since his visit, and pray he will appear soon again.

> *A dream is a wish your heart makes—*
> *When you're fast asleep.*

MEDITATION FORTY-ONE

Volare oh oh

Let's fly way up in the clouds, away from the maddening crowds.

—from the song *Volare oh oh*

My Dad had various cars while I was growing up and after. Since I am not knowledgeable about cars, I cannot relate much in their regard. I will always remember though he bought a new popular model of a Studebaker back in the 1950s that was of such a design you could not tell whether it was coming or going. And it was bright red! Now this car was so out of character for him in every way, that it amazed me, and frankly, I cannot image my Mother agreeing to it yet I know he would not have bought it if she had not agreed. He did not have it very long, but it was fun while he owned it. All his other cars were so sedate and unusual I do not even remember them except one. Maybe they were all the same one except for this special one. I just cannot tell you.

The one that has meaning for me was an attractive pale shade of green, like the trees in our woods and it was a Plymouth Volare. I thought the car was really special and I liked its name because I enjoyed the song that was on the charts in that era and long before and after made popular by Dean Martin—*Volare, oh oh, Volare, oh oh.* My Uncle Elmer, my Mother's brother who passed away three months after my Dad, bought a dark blue Volare at the same time as my Dad. It was the same model and year. When my Uncle passed, my Mother eventually sold his car and his home, yet not immediately. But my Mother kept the green Volare of Dad's even though she did not drive. When she went to Heaven the next year the Volare became ours. For a long time it just sat in one of

148

our garages. For me it seemed as yet untouchable. It was too fresh from my Dad. I would look in its windows in the garage and cry. I never got inside it.

Finally after two years, our son began attending Villanova University and eventually needed a car as he commuted the first two years. The first year I was involved in his transportation and this was a very long drive from our home. I drove my van, not the Volare. The second year we decided George could use the Volare. The third and fourth year he lived on campus and the Volare was back in our garage. One day I began to drive it. Almost all my married life I had driven vans, the type that were very large, seated eight, and did not look like the vans of today. Over a period of many years as our family grew in number and height we had three vans in succession, a pale blue Ford, a green Chevy, and a black and white 1978 Ford we bought in 1980 and it is still sitting here at the top of our hill here in the woods. Though not running now, we still have not parted with it due to my sentimentality. That van represents all three vans to me and my years of driving them filled with singing children and tapes I played in the van, music that I was addicted to and that would cause the kids to sing more and to sing louder so I would not play them endlessly. But they did enjoy a lot of that music too. The vans represented fun and family and of course were used for vacations, and at those times they were driven by Bob. Our three Cairn Terriers also enjoyed these family trips.

But once I began to drive the Volare, it became unique and I began to drive it when alone. I continued to use the van when driving with the family and transporting them here and there, but when I attended daily Mass and went out on errands alone, I always drove my Dad's Volare. I really liked it, and too, it had incredible wide vision with a higher front seat and a front window like our van's, so large and open. Other sedan cars we have had since do not. They require me to pull the seat up so close to the steering wheel because of my height and in order to see over the steering wheel properly that cuts the vision. (our daughter Barbie said to me if she was in the front with me on occasion—*"What are you, Mom, an elf?"*)

The Volare was lovely and I truly enjoyed being alone in it often imagining my Dad seated where I now was. Only two incidents occurred with it after it became mine and they were memorable. One on March

20, 1986 is related in the first chapter of my book *The Enchantment of Writing* that involved a near fatal accident while I was in it and waiting for a light to change at a busy intersection in Darby, Pennsylvania. I was flanked by cars on both sides hoping to eventually make a turn when a car appeared straight ahead of me across Lansdowne Avenue with sirens screaming and lights flashing. It came out of nowhere and I could not move due to the other cars. I closed my eyes and waited for the impact believing I was about to die. I had no fear. None!

But it did not hit! Only God could have intervened and allowed that police car to pass me in some supernatural way, for there was absolutely no passage. When I opened my eyes I was still alive! I will not relate all that I wrote about that incident but what amazed me was my calmness of spirit as I was about to die. God alone transported that speeding police car that had no place to go except into the front of Dad's Volare, to somewhere behind me. I could not comprehend it all as I continued driving to St. Francis House, my destination, nor did I seem rattled or shaken. This is what amazed me, my calmness of spirit. God had given me a complete peace before the incident as I waited to be crushed head on, and afterwards as I sat there whole.

Like the symbolism of the statue we gave my Dad after his larynx removal, of the child in the Lord's Hand, it would seem He truly holds you in His Hand at moments such as these. Had this been my time to die I would have met death in peace and completely unafraid. Also as I look back on all of this, my Dad too could have interceded in some way prayerfully or otherwise as his daughter was about to be hit head-on as she sat in his car. I am a safe driver and have never had any drivers' violation tickets or accidents in my history. This was a once in a lifetime happening.

Following that incident a new peace flowed through me, for I sensed that insight had been given to me that I was spiritually ready to die. This comforts me though I may have not interpreted it correctly. Three months later almost to the day, dear Rochester would enter my life. I needed to be here to receive him forever.

Later I would have one more incident in our (Dad's and mine) Volare within the next year or two. I cannot remember the exact time though I know it is recorded in a journal. I was returning in mid-evening from this same St. Francis House in Darby and due to the very long drive home to

Jenkintown, I occasionally stopped at a 7-11 store to buy a large cup of coffee to accompany me as I did on this particular night. I returned to my car and started to back out, and as I did there was a large thud under the car and whatever had happened caused the car to be immobile. I looked underneath and saw something had dropped out of the body of the car but was still attached by one end inside of it. A telephone booth was outside the store and I called home to Bob to tell what occurred and to ask advice. He said it was the drive shaft from my description and that we would have to wait to get it fixed. He asked me to take a cab home. I had only money for coffee, and a little gas if I needed it. Not much. I told the person in the store who had waited on me that I would have to leave the car there and why. I headed outside again knowing I had to call a taxi. As I came out the door a taxi actually drove in and parked next to my Volare! (I always feel like singing that song when I write that name) God and Dad had seemingly intervened again for my Volare and me! I went to the open window of the cab and told the driver my dilemma. He was so nice. You see, I doubt if any driver at that time of night, except myself, felt like driving that long way to Jenkintown and have to go through so much traffic on busy roads. It was always a long ride I enjoyed alone with time for thoughts and prayers and quiet classical music, often *Vivaldi's Four Seasons*. But when I told him my destination he was dumbfounded! I can still see the surprise on his face. He then told me that he had just talked to the operator of his taxi base and told her he would like to take a long ride and that maybe she could find him someone who wanted to go to Jenkintown!! Naturally I though he was teasing me, but he called into his operator and simply asked her to repeat what he had just requested of her. The woman's voice came through confirming he had requested Jenkintown! Now I was really in awe! How could God or Dad not have arranged that request and put that desire in the drivers mind? Of all places he could choose to go—why the far away tiny town of Jenkintown?

And so I got in the cab after locking the Volare and with coffee in hand I listened to tale after tale of a cab driver's adventures as we drove that long distance to the place that driver wanted to visit. And he knew I had barely any money. He trusted me. It was a ride I have always remembered, a strange ride with a big stranger, but a very big hearted jovial one. Once home, I took him in the house like he was a long-time buddy and introduced him to Bob. He was rather like my hero! By now I felt like he was a true friend.

And so after Bob paid him a huge amount of money (neither of us remember the exact amount but it was approximately, and no less than, ninety dollars plus a fine tip) I bid my rescuer goodbye. Not every taxi driver would have said yes to the destination I had requested, but this driver I believe had had his destination whispered to him before he met and rescued me.

The next day Bob and I went back to Darby together to rescue the Volare, but in obtaining a reliable and knowledgeable auto mechanic we learned that the Volare should not be repaired, that there were many other things within it on the brink of failing and beyond repair. It was time to retire my Dad's and my wonderful Volare, travelling friend of many years. It was not an easy moment when I had to walk away and know I would never see again this object and friend of great meaning for me. Yes, I had tears. I consider this Volare an Earth Angel, a term i have come to know through a wonderful book and that I have mentioned in other writings, and a gift from my Dad. It was the end of an era. Unlike his tie clasp and ring that can forever remain with me until I join him, it would not have been so for the Volare *unless* we towed it up here to New Hampshire to sit beside our Chevy Van and let it spend all of its days in our lovely green woods. An authoritative man, totally unsentimental about cars, and who paid my huge taxi fare and a towing charge in Darby to remove the Volare from in front of a 7-11—said NO!

> The car can also influence spiritual contemplation, the car becomes a beloved partner, a means of transport that is not restricted to physical movement. He unites himself with the car, travels and glows with its spirit. He loses himself in its being.
>
> —Shaun McNiff, *Earth Angels: Engaging the Sacred in Everyday Things*

Please, when you read the above quotation, replace the words "he" and "himself" with "she" and "herself." This quotation is speaking of myself.

When Bob learned I was writing about my Dad's Volare, he looked up information about it online. To me it is interesting enough to include for we never knew anything about it before, other than it ran very well and had a nice appearance. Most unusual knowledge to me is that is was only produced for five years from 1976 through 1980 by the Chrysler Corporation's Dodge division that also produced the Dodge Aspen. The Plymouth Volare and the Dodge Aspen were collectively named Motor Trend's *"Car of the Year"* for 1976. My Dad had the four-door model as did my Uncle. I now have learned through this information that my Dad bought the car in 1976 as did my Uncle, for they obtained them at the same time, the first year of the car's production, or possibly in January of 1977. In February of 1977 my Dad's life changed with his larynx operation as I have written, and both men pass away later that same year. Neither bought cars from February, 1977 on. I did not realize the car was so new when it came into our possession in September 1978 for it is not something I would give importance to in my thinking.

Even though the car grew to have a sweetness and great significance to it simply because it was my Dad's, I knew nothing about it as a car—only as a former container of my Dad's physical presence. He had sat in the seat where I was sitting and his hands had held that same wheel. I realize now it was an "Earth Angel" and an entity of love holding me until the arrival of my angel from Heaven in soft marmalade fur. The Volare had been on earth ten years and died a month before Rochester's birth. Two months later Rochester would enter my life.

It is remarkable how the presence of a thing can change the structure of our lives.

—Shaun McNiff, *Earth Angels*

Nel Blu, Dipinto di Blu (Volare)

Though the lovely song Volare had been especially made popular by Dean Martin for me and millions of others, it was also made a hit by Frank Sinatra and others in different years. All the lyrics to the song and a history of it can be obtained online.

The lyrics are in Italian but partially translated and sung in English too. It is written it is the first foreign language single to top the charts in the rock era. *Billboard Magazine* declared it number one for the year 1958. That is when Dean Martin hit the charts with it.

The title *Volare* translates to *The Blue (Sky)*, *Painted in Blue* and "*Volare*" to fly. Dominco Modugno co-wrote it with Franco Migliacci after Modugno described a man's dream of flying through the air with his hands painted blue. Modugno's only United States hit was Volare which was number one for five weeks in 1958. Modugno performed the song for the first time at the Sanremo Song Festival in Italy, where he won first prize.

All of the lyrics of the many verses in English and Italian are lovely (to me) and the music. I leave you with a few lines. Perhaps you too remember them.

> *Volare, oh oh, contare, oh oh oh oh*
> *Let's fly way up to the clouds, away from the maddening crowds*
> *We can sing in the glow of a star that I know of*
> *Where lovers enjoy peace of mind*
> *Let us leave the confusion and all disillusion behind*
> *Just like bird of a feather, a rainbow together we'll find*
> *Volare, oh oh, e contare, oh oh oh oh*

MEDITATION FORTY-TWO

How Deep Is His Love

When you are dead
seek for your resting place
not in the earth
but in the hearts of men.

—Rumi

As I tell elsewhere, my Dad is very real and present to me. It is my Dad as well as Mary, our Blessed Mother, that I ask to take care of my beloved Rochester until I join them in Heaven. therefore, my Rochester belongs in my Dad's book just as my Dad is in Rochester's. My Dad loves and cares about our family cat, Mitzi, so deeply when I am growing up, as do I, that twenty-one years after Mitzi's death, and following my Dad's and Mother's deaths thirteen months apart, I learn a precious secret. My Dad's wallet and little notebook he always carries become mine. Inside the notebook encircled by a fat rubberband on a small neatly folded paper, I discover how deep is his love for Mitzi. Even the rubber band stands the test of time. I hold this paper of his in my hand now. In four months it will be fifty-one years old. Written in his neat small handwriting are these words.

WEDNESDAY
August 22nd—1956
at 8:30 PM
Mitzi

He carries this paper for twenty-one years until his own death when he joins Mitzi in Heaven! These words of his record Mitzi's departure, the time and day and date.

He dies August 21st, one day before she does, but over two decades later. I know he is grief stricken, and I too share his grief. I keep the little paper with his treasured handwriting and words in a lovely treasure box on my desk for all these years.

I honor my Dad even more for his love of Mitzi and his continuing sorrow over her death. Mitzi, a beautiful little affectionate black Persian, appears in my books *Enchantment of Writing* and *Compassion for All Creatures* through word and a small picture. The same picture in color and framed is in our living room this day and has been for many years.

Along with the small memorial to Mitzi on paper, my Dad also carries a drawing I make for him. As a child there are two little characters I love to draw just for fun, and for some reason they amuse my Dad also. One is a shmoo, an endearing little creature created and drawn by artist Al Capp and who appears in his famous comic strip "Lil Abner." The other is a strange little man I create with long legs and knobby knees and big shoes,

a man with head thrown back and a long nose in the air and mouth wide open with musical notes drawn in a cloud near his head indicating as is done with comic strip characters that the notes are coming from the large circle mouth on his face. The little singing man is the drawing he carries.

This is a pencil sketch I made of my Dad when I was 14 and he was 43. I used to sketch and draw all the time, but unfortunately this is one of the few that have survived.

As the years pass, I realize how very much I am like him emotionally, and in cherishing beings and memories and tangible keepsakes of theirs. That he needs to put into writing his deep sorrow for Mitzi, though only a few words, tells in a brief cameo what I am trying to express in writing this book. His few words speak volumes.

MITZI

Mitzi joined our family
Constantly she stayed with me.
By my side as I would write
Snuggled close she'd sleep each night!
Marriage caused us then to part
I had to leave her—break her heart!
My parents wanted her to stay
They needed her—I was away.

from my poem   Jan
Feline Family   May 3, 1991
3rd verse

Mitzi too adored my Dad—
She'd cheer him up when he was sad.
Their mutual love was special grace
She'd sit and gaze into his face—
And cuddle close upon his lap
Together they would take a nap.
For she was one of Dad's "three girls"
The sweet short black one with no curls.

For sweet Mitzi   Jan
                                                 July 14, 2007

A tender little postscript to the sharing of Mitzi's life entwined with that of my Dad's is that some years after the demise of the treasured green Volare of my Dad's we bought a now old but very cute and reliable small Sport Expo Mitsubishi car that I drive. This 1992 model bought in 1993 we named Mitzi. Though she is bright red and not black, I believe our sweet Mitzi is pleased and honored this namesake bought in New Hampshire has been part of us here in the woods for fourteen years. Maybe it was Mitzi who influenced my Dad to buy that crazy little red Studebaker back in the 1950s.

Mitzi

Holy and Sustaining Beliefs

I think death is a tremendous adventure—a gateway into a new life, in which you have further powers.

—Dr. Leslie D. Weatherhead

There are many passages in books I read and inspiring quotations. I have recorded many of them through the years in special journals just for my own inspiration and before I ever begin to write books of my own. But in the years since Rochester passed, there were even significantly more that just moved me so , and I needed them with all my heart. Three writings in particular were given to me by God and Rochester within the first months of Rochester's passing. They were like food and water to someone who was dying within in grief. I remember the moments in which I read each for the first time separated by only short spans of days because I was reading continuously. Each struck at my soul and pierced it forever with sustaining never before heard words as if from another world. To this moment whenever I think of them or reread them, they still have the same precious affect and impact upon me and bring tears. I will tell you of them now and leave them upon my pages in case you too need messages from beyond.

They are all shared in the first book of my Trilogy *In Corridors of Eternal Time*, but also may be mentioned in the other two.

The first is a wondrous thought.

What if you slept? And what if, in your sleep, you dreamed? And what if, in your dream, you went to heaven and there plucked a strange and beautiful flower? And what if, when you awoke, you had the flower in your hand? Ah, what then?

This is an invitation to reconsider your thoughts about reality and to examine your imagination. It asks you to consider what you are capable of and what is possible in your dream state. This can apply to visions also. They are interconnected. Written by one of the world's renowned poets, theologians and philosophers, Samuel Taylor Coleridge, the poem strikes my heart. I believe that with God all things are possible! What I have written on these pages I believe expresses my heart and soul and deep beliefs and that miracles occur, and that Rochester lives and is ever here. And I believe my Dad is also. I believe that it is possible to hold a flower in my hand that I plucked from a garden in my dreams. Samuel Taylor Coleridge believes it to be also.

Since I first encountered this passage wondrous interconnections with Rochester have occurred that I would never have thought possible before his passing.

Upon nearing completion writing my book *Corridors*, I discovered a poem by the great poet Rumi—a man from another time and place. It left me weak to read it and just blew me away. It was as if a portion of the poem was written for Rochester and me, and that he knew what we are experiencing in our life together day by day. I left the poem on a page quite near the beginning of *Corridors* even though I was not yet finished writing when I discovered the passage by Rumi. It seemed important to place it exactly where I did and not at the end of my book. Here it is now for you.

> *You must ask for what you really want.*
> *Don't go back to sleep.*
> *People are going back and forth*
> *Across the doors where the two worlds touch.*
> *The door is round and open.*
> *Don't go back to sleep.*
>
> —Rumi

I pray this blesses you.

My last little sharing is in regard to all the happenings that occurred in my life through Rochester following his entrance into Heaven and in regard to the happenings that continue to occur. I had opened a new book at random that day in 2002 and on the page saw the following words indented. They read:

> *Where there is a profound revelation, in the very recognition that "this is revelation" you have to become serious about your own life. The instant you recognize that you are seeing the truth as it is you must realize the implications of what is being revealed to you.*

The author goes on to say that your confidence in that revelation can only grow stronger if it is not betrayed even once. He states that the stronger the confidence, then the deeper will be your wisdom. But he warns that if you carelessly or needlessly engage in or allow yourself to indulge in doubt, then your confidence will be undermined for you are walking down a precarious road. The author of these words is Andrew Cohen from his book, *Enlightenment Is a Secret*. I am not familiar with the writer but the statement appears in a book by an author that I have read many times and heard on Maine Public Television, Dr. Wayne W. Dyer. This statement is in his book, *Your Sacred Self*.

I have never allowed my revelations in regard to Rochester (whom I was speaking about in *Corridors* for it was written for him) nor more recently in regard to my Dad, to be undermined. I have never wavered from my beliefs or doubted any gifts of spirit or revelation given to me. I have never allowed myself to be undermined, nor betrayed any wisdom, insights or contacts. I believe my beliefs and doubt my doubts, words from a hymn Bob wrote years ago. I cannot begin to tell you the strength of this wisdom. I do not waver.

I pray these three passages are spiritual gifts to you in some incredible way as they continue to be to me.

> *If you love the truths that you find in your soul, do not abandon them because someone outside of your soul does not agree with them or ridicules or questions them. You are not saying that your truth is THE truth. You are saying that it is YOUR truth.*
>
> —Neale Donald Walsch, *Home with God In a Life That Never Ends*

> *Accept death as a door, not a wall.*
>
> —Louis LaGrand, Ph.D

MEDITATION FORTY-FOUR

Everywhere

As I write these words and as I near completion of this book and am about to proofread, it is two weeks after Rochester's May 30th birthday and one week and three days from my Dad's of June 2nd. The meditations I give to you now that follow these words are Holy meditations to me that I spontaneously write for two of my previous books. The latter one is written five years ago in June 2002, three months following Rochester's entrance into Heaven. It is all truth of my soul that expresses exactly how I feel then and am ever the same in the present and forevermore.

The one that precedes it and follows this explanatory writing, is written four years ago. It is emphasizing the beauty and truth of the earlier meditation and to hopefully minister to any readers who too may be grieving or who simply are, during this period, keeping company with Ellis and Rochester.

> *If your mind is closed, you cannot learn anything new. Closed minds reject anything different, anything that conflicts with their old beliefs, beliefs that may be false. They have forgotten that experience is stronger than belief. Fear is the force that keeps minds closed. Only open minds can receive and process new knowledge.*
>
> —Brian Weiss, M.D.

JUNE 28, 2003

In proofreading my previous book *In Corridors of Eternal Time* for my publisher I am in tears. While reading it I realize that it is a strength to me, my very own words. For you see these words were written one year and one week ago today, and all that I read in this meditational journal entry I can rewrite this very moment with the same conviction and say to you that it is completely true. I have lived one more year of life and without the physical presence of my beloved Rochester. It still feels as if it is last year this time for I am living in the present moment continually as if Rochester just left. I prayed this would be so, so that I might live on the brink of two worlds. God has answered my prayer. I live life still with Rochester, except he is in spirit. My grief is as intense as I prayed it always would be. The words written in the meditation that follows will further make this clear. I am living out the truth of this gift.

I pray that if you should ever lose a beloved animal or human that you will not relegate your beloved one to the past, be ashamed of grieving, and move on, not keeping your beloved very present to you. Often grieving is seen as a weakness. It is not! It is a precious strength! Only until you realize it in its full capacity as I have and have others, and allow it to be an integral and enormous part of who you are now and every shall be, will you truly ever know who you yourself really are and experience this transformation. May the meditation that follows speak to your heart and soul.

Everywhere

He had ceased to meet us in particular places
in order to meet us everywhere.

—C.S. Lewis

FRIDAY, JUNE 21, 2002

The love I shared and still share forever with Rochester is a gift. I carry this grief gladly, for without it would mean I had never had Rochester in my life. It is a gift from our one life lived together. I cannot ever comprehend life without Rochester, and I would not trade one moment of this sorrow, even with all the pain, in contrast to never having lived and loved with Rochester. It was a spiritual dimension of living that defies explanation, and now it continues on still yet another plane until we are together in Heaven. Without Rochester I cannot imagine what the past almost sixteen years would have been.

Perhaps there are some who have lost human or animal companion loved ones who wonder where their loved ones are. Please pray and find a peace in the certainty that they live on. I am secure in my belief of sharing life with Rochester in Heaven, and that my Dad is caring for him until I join them. Yet I know too, as many do, that my loved one is still here with me, for I experience him and sense him. His spirit never deserts me, never departs. He is around me, beside me, within me, and slumbers on my legs. This will always be so. It is an unfathomable comfort. It is a solace beyond words.

Losing my loved one's physical presence changed me. I see the world differently, and a sense of solid individualism has strengthened me. I do not have to answer to others about my grief. I am changed internally, spiritually, and in mysterious ways. There is a new person within that has stronger beliefs and an endurance level I did not know was ever possible. I believe Rochester's Anima, his breath and soul within me, his eternal gift to me, is this underlying strength. And yes, God's grace,—and His Holy Spirit bestowed on me at conception. I have resources and power within me that rise up and sustain even in my most anguished moments of depletion, and of experiencing Rochester's physical absence. I believe it is my most devastating loss, yet I know it is imparting a wisdom to carry

*Rochester on his wildlife quilt made by Janna
on the bed in our writing/prayer room.*

me through what days of my life I have left until I am in Heaven with
Rochester. The life we had together cannot be duplicated. It was and is
a divine gift. Both Rochester and I are transformed. You who read may
come to know this transformation too, if you are deeply grieving for one
who was and is a special world unto itself for you alone.

EVERYWHERE

He is near
My little dear—
He is far
He is my Star.

He is without
He is within—
In the silence
In the din.

He sustains
He ordains—
Removes fear
He is here.

For eternal   Jan
Rochester

Another Friday. Another Holy Hour from 5 to 6 PM in solitude,
remembrance, prayer, tears, and eternal love. He is here.

MEDITATION FORTY-FIVE

Conversations

Our relationship with the departed is not over; it has just changed
dimensions. Keep talking to them, and don't be surprised if you seem
to hear them answer—This silent heart speech may last a lifetime.

—Stephen Levine, *Unattended Sorrow*

Talking to my loved ones in Heaven is not an unusual occurrence to me. It is part of my life—night and day I have so many precious conversations and sharings with them that I often have to be reeled in from the ether and back to the real world. But who is to say which is the real world? I believe it is all one world just different dimensional. Talking to our loved ones is beautiful to do and too, to expect answers. I do receive answers and others do also. Be sure to write everything down in your journal, it will become a reference and guide for you on your journey. It is comforting to read especially in moments when you become sad and downcast and are missing the physical presence of those you love.

Stephen Levine writes of heart speech so eloquently in his book *Unattended Sorrow*, another book that I have read multiple times and go back into frequently just to be comforted by certain chapters.He tells us that we speak into another's heart as an expansion of our own continued healing. We use this practicing of connecting with another silently, feeling as one might when singing a child to sleep and it soothes us. When someone first passes away it is lovely to utilize heart speech to send blessings directly from your heart to your loved one's heart. One can do this also if a loved one is in a coma such as my Mother was in her last hours. We stood by her and whispered loving thoughts and prayers and talked to her softly aloud. We believe she heard us.

We cannot know the invaluableness of heart speech to those who have passed over into the light but it truly helps the sender. It has helped me tremendously and maintained a preciousness of union. The author tells in his book of a former teacher of his whom he constantly had great difficulty in reaching by phone, yet after the man's death he writes that they speak now more often than ever and Stephen receives precious guidance from him. He emphasizes he can reach his friend on the *heartline* anytime he wishes. And this has been so for years for Rochester and myself, and for me to read it often in my journals and in this book gives great confirmation and consolation to myself anew and hopefully to readers.

This author also writes so tenderly of tapping the heart and it is a gentle practice I began after the first reading of this book in 2005. He suggests gently tapping your heart to call it out of the shadows. This can be done while still or in rhythm with walking. If our heart is numb due to a beloved one's passing the tapping can help to awaken it. Some massage small circles over their grief points or press it lightly with their thumb while remembering their love and loss. He writes it is as if a small sacred circle can still be felt circumscribing the heart after we take our hand away. It is a loving, loving practice of connecting to your loved one in your heart and I believe you will be blessed and helped. I have been doing heart speech since my parents passed years ago, but just not calling it by that lovely name, but much much more do I do it with Rochester after his passing. Tapping the heart is a newer practice learned through this fine book two years ago.

How beautiful and appropriate is the quotation by Antoine de-Saint-Exupery that I have shared in a previous book and elsewhere in this one. He states, *"It is with the heart that one sees rightly; what is essential is invisible to the eye." Another author writes "If you see a heart, think of your loved ones hearts, so full of love for you still, waiting to show us on that glorious day all the wonders they already know in heaven, where love begins and never ends."* (Unknown)

Many messages sent to us are often not received because we do not pay attention. We believe touches from the spirit world and loved ones are our imagination and do not trust that first intuitive burst of knowingness. As a prayerful person try to trust and believe in the thoughts that come to you and have faith in the first impressions you receive. Often we receive sweet unexpected contacts from our loved ones and what if you missed one? Somehow when a loving contact is made you have *"know-ing,"* and as written in other meditations in this book they can come in many ways and are such incredible blessings.

Louis LeGrand, Ph.D—author of several books on Afterlife, (*After Death Communications, Messages and Miracles*) states in his book *Love Lives On* that Catholics and Protestant denominations embrace the belief that those who die can be prayed to directly for guidance, advice, even for help, and that people who are grieving the loss of a loved one—even if they are not of these faiths or do not believe in a Higher Power—should consider taking the idea to heart. He relates how we can still be greatly effected by our loved one's continued presence and learn a great deal from his or her advice. He encourages us to ask questions and carefully consider their opinions. He states that soon you will find insights coming out of nowhere. I have been living in this way for five years and can only say amen to his words.

Each precious *"Hello from Heaven"* sustains, enriches and helps us to carry on and travel our journey, and authors Bill Guggenheim and Judy Guggenheim have written a book by this title and collected countless true *"Hellos"* for its pages given them by strangers who have experienced such love from beyond in many forms from their loved ones in Heaven. It is one of the first books I read on this subject and have gone back to it often.

Author Sinclair Browning in her lovely book of true stories of Mothers connecting with their daughters and titled *"Feathers Brush My Heart"* tells us to trust and believe in the thoughts that come to you and have faith in first impressions and while we may not be able to summon communications at will, it certainly does not hurt to ask. And I do and Rochester responds regularly to my prayers for him. Often we receive a touch from a loved one even when we have not specifically asked and I can attest to that and all else I have written in this meditation. Unexpected communications are such gifts. All touches are. This author believes in making requests out loud in contrast to others who do it silently in their heart. Each person can find their own way of sending love and words to the person that is their precious one and whom they love and miss with all that is within them. In regard to afterlife gifts, there is no right or wrong way to receive or send a gift of love. You will know. Just trust your heart thoughts and feelings. Our loved ones hear and are always with us. Their communications come in many forms—just as Rochester's communications come to me.

Last Night
I spoke your name to the wind
which told the trees,
which touched the sky,
which shone with moonlight,
which filled my world
with dreams of you.

—Unknown

MEDITATION FORTY-SIX

A Parentless Parent

Overnight I had become a parentless parent.

—Allison Gilbert

Often a person who has lost a parent or both parents when they are younger, or early middle age as I was, makes a drastic change in their life. It can come in many ways. It is written frequently how one will change their religion or give it up altogether. In my life as I have revealed, I left the Methodist Church for the Catholic Church following my parents passing and within only three months of my Mother's, who was the last one to leave.

Another writer who made such a religious change simply stopped going to synagogue because she associated her religion with her parents and had always gone to synagogue with them. Over time she achieved her own way of finding peace. She goes to a bookstore and browses for hours or to an Art Museum or listens to music. In combination with my attending church, I too needed book stores and books and do to this day. I used to say when living in Jenkintown, that bookstores were my "second church" and would go to one or the other of the two in town often following daily Mass in the mornings or after confession on Saturday nights. Music too has always had enormous meaning for me through the years as I have written frequently and in more detail in other books. But following the passing of Rochester it was painful to listen to any music at all and still to this day I prefer the silence and sounds of nature and bird song here in the woods. Though art was a part of my life as a teenager and younger person I do not visit museums now. But a number of times a year I visit the Walden book store 25 miles from here in Rochester that has special meaning for me in regard to my Rochester, and at least twice a year, and always one of those times on my birthday, we go to Newington, 50 miles from our home, to the huge Barnes and Noble there. It becomes my vestibule to Heaven as I remain at least five hours and browse and purchase books on the only subjects now I can study and read—for I am being led on a path that leaves no desire for variances.

Writing and reading poetry became enormously important to me in the mid-eighties when Rochester entered my life. I have written of this in more detail in my previous book *Cherishing*. This love of poetry continues to this moment and ministers to me. I once wrote poetry on every subject that affected my life and when Rochester entered it poems never stopped streaming out of me for him and never shall. I did not write poems for my Dad—or Mother—until after the mid-eighties. So many poems to help myself, I wrote, but so many too will never ever be in any of my books.

Since Rochester's passing my poetry changed. And like an author I have referred to here, the poems I like to read now are not happy poems. They are sad. I prefer poems that attempt to express the same feelings I am experiencing or similar. Reading happy poems does not help. I keep a poem book in the car. Poetry brings me solace. Another writer I have read recently also states how poetry and journal writing help her to deal with her pain. She feels each can send you on a journey to find out what you are feeling. Yes, I have been on a journey and will ever continue to be on one.

But too, you learn how strong you are in times of loss. Learning that you are capable of enduring is a strength. Another woman writer states that friends and family do not always understand why she is still sad. They feel she should be fine now; it has been years. Like myself she thinks people need to be more sensitive to the fact that the loss remains active for the rest of your life. It does not go away; it just changes.

My parents left me while I was in process. I had just begun to evolve from a single adult to married woman with children.—They left me with many questions unanswered. They left me before I was old enough to be left.

—Allison Gilbert from *Always Too Soon: Voices of Support for Those Who Have Lost Both Parents*

A Gift for Eternity

Eternal Gift

You send me pennies
From on high—
I leave you pennies
In reply —

Outside the store
I lay each down—
Upon a sill
Within the town—

Where God placed you
And I a plea —
To take you home
That day with me.

But through those pleadings —
We could not foresee —
That together we are spending
Eternity!

Thank you, God!

For my dear Rochester on his birthday   Jan
May 30, 2007
with eternal love

Upon first reading the poem that opens this meditation one might not fully understand the words "plea" and "pleadings" in the context of the message of this poem. I will briefly try to explain in a short passage taken from a chapter in my book *Compassion For All Creatures*. Rochester was the inspiration for that book as he was and is for all books I write. I titled that first chapter *"We Meet and the Angels Sing."* I believe that will help you to understand my joy. The Angels continue to sing in our eternal bond and ever shall and Rochester is ever my joy.

We Meet and the Angels Sing!

I love these little people: and it is not a slight thing when they, who are so fresh from God, love us."

—Charles Dickens

The black and white van pulled into the very large parking lot of a very ordinary little mall in Rochester, New Hampshire. It was late morning of a bright and beautiful day in June and my husband and I smiled and commented on the blessing of our safe arrival. We slowly opened the doors, slid down from our seats and out of the van. Our teenage daughter, Janna, rolled gracefully out from the side door with her curly hair going in various directions and her expression still one of drowsiness. We had travelled through the night from our home in Pennsylvania and this stop was only to quickly buy groceries. We would take them with us to our cottage on Lake Balch some twenty-five miles further north.

As we entered the mall we were immediately confronted with a father—and two children sitting on a round bench outside the supermarket and holding a sign that read—"Free Kittens." Next to them on the bench was a closed carton. My daughter and I, upon encountering this sight, widened our eyes in a spontaneous secret signal to each other without my husband realizing what was about to befall him.

Now, lest you begin to feel sorry for my husband—let me hurriedly take you back many years in order to understand the scene that has been unraveling before your eyes. I had been born into a home with a cat and had grown up with cats. Until I married and left home exactly upon turning twenty-one years—I had had the joy and companionship of cats. But the day I married Bob—he said emphatically "No Cats!"

In my thirty-two years of marriage I had loved and reared six children; five wonderful daughters and a fine son. I had also loved and cared for three hardy and adorable little Cairn Terriers and all the puppies of their many litters. This also included a vacation when we travelled to New Hampshire with nine dogs and five children and an infant girl. One of the dogs had had six puppies the night before we were to leave and so they too had to vacation with us so that they might be close to their Mother and be properly nourished.

There had also been hamsters during those thirty-two years, and guinea pigs, mice, turtles, gerbils, fish—and one hermit crab that was lost in our home.

All of these—but my husband had said—"No Cats!"

Occasionally throughout these many years I had asked if I might have a kitten. More recently our daughter Janna had voiced the same request. Always the answer came back—"No Cats!"

Ah—but this day in the mall in New Hampshire some supernatural power took over within me as I made my first pleas to Bob—in order that Janna and I might have one of these free kittens. When his usual reply came back to me accompanied by the expression on his face I well recognized—I would not be silenced! I asked again. Again. AGAIN. I began to frighten myself in my persistence that refused to buckle under his rising anger and stormy appearance. I could not quiet my pleas until I at last—after thirty-two years—had won my simple request. Nothing else mattered in those moments but a "yes." I could never again bear to hear—"No Cats!"

"Alright, alright—get one—but I'll have nothing to do with it," he hissed. I began to say a continuous stream of "thank yous" and ran off to find my daughter who had delicately removed herself earlier from the muffled battle scene. Oh, the joy and excitement of the two of us—as we stifled squeals of victory between us there in the aisle of the supermarket.

Perhaps now you can understand my reference to the words "plea" and "pleading." I was delirious with happiness with my dear little kitten. There is much more to that story of the entrance of Rochester into my life, into *our* lives, and of course he completely won Bob over. One can read about it and so much more concerning all forms of compassion in that second book of mine. A handsome portrait of Rochester is on the cover.

I will always remember seeing at least a dozen copies of my *Compassion* interspersed with copies of *Higher Ground* in the largest store window of Bookland in Stanford, Maine—a store I shopped in faithfully every two weeks. Cheryl, a young saleswoman who always talked with me and we shared in common many things, loved my books and she continually promoted them. There were also numerous displays of them inside the store and the ones in the window remained for months until Bookland ceased to be and the chain of stores closed. I also had two booksignings there. It was a significant and lovely period and I felt I was also helping others come to know Rochester and the importance of dear animals in humans' lives. I will always be appreciative of Cheryl's friendship.

Rochester did not only become my companion but truly became my Angel.

To Bob he became *Harry* and warmed Bob's heart and won for himself his own acceptance through his continued silence and his unconditional love. Bob does not conform, or rarely, and though he thought Rochester and Chester exceptional names he needed still another that he alone called him.

I believe it was all a part of God's great plan to send Rochester to me for after I had entered the Catholic Church following my Dad's and Mother's entrance into Heaven, life had become far, far less than heavenly on earth for me. I was made to feel less, and though I did not enter the Catholic Church without first having full permission from Bob and our children, there was an on-going enormous affliction upon and within our family and very especially upon me. It has been written about in my first book *Higher Ground*, a book that was the outcome of a journal I kept on that retreat of one week spent here in our cottage alone with only Rochester as a kitten. We did not yet live in New Hampshire permanently. But it was not written about in entirety, just in a veiled way in order to protect persons involved. I know the book helped and still helps many despite the fact a mystery has remained and extremely personal details cannot be told. There is sufficient revelation within its pages that it does the spiritual work for others it is intended to do. And it helped me enormously to write it.

My spirituality has deepened even more so and changed since the passing of Rochester for I have been shown much and truly blessed. Where once and for years I used to keep a little ringed plaque by my phone with words of Eleanor Roosevelt that said *"No one can make you feel inferior without your consent"* (for my middle name has been "inferior"). I now have slowly gone through a metamorphosis. Rochester's life and passing and continual presence have given me an inner strength and a spirituality of never-ending hope and the joy and belief of full reunions with Rochester and Dad and my other loved ones in Heaven. I am now too learning to feel worthy of this high calling.

When Rochester entered my life everything negative did not disappear, the afflictions and troubles existing in my life, but he gave me a new way of living in spirit and I grew stronger. And I wrote and wrote our books and journals as he kept company with me through all his days and nights, *our* days and nights, and does so still in spirit. I know God sent Rochester to that bench in the Mall that day of June 23, 1986, but I see now too, after all the writing of this book, that there is the enormous possibility my Dad interceded and asked God to send him to me. He understood and knew how I needed a precious and dear little angel like Rochester in my life just as he and I shared the love and comfort of Mitzi in previous years of both sorrows and joys. Yes, I believe he did whisper that request to God.

The poem that begins this meditation was written in the car before placing the penny spoken of on the sill for Rochester's Birthday. The poem seemed to flow out. The poem that follows was given to me when I arrived home and was still in the spiritual aura of visiting that Holy place.

His Green Glass Jar

It is five years now
That I come to this store—
Leaving you pennies
As I've done before.

And you send me pennies
I protect in a jar—
They are pennies from Heaven
And you are my Star.

May 30, 2007   —Jan
For my Sweet Rochester

I will be returning to place another penny on June 23rd, the anniversary of the day he entered my life twenty-one years ago. After leaving the penny for his birthday we went to Home Depot next door in the outdoor Mall to the store where the penny lay on the sill. I picked out a gorgeous purple hydrangea bush as Chester's new memory plant this year. The blooms and green foliage are our two favorite colors. Too, I bought petunias and begonias for his gardens. My thoughts were filled with memories of him as we stood in a long line in the huge hothouse of flowers and shrubs. Suddenly the background music on the public address system that I had been trying to ignore, changed. The familiar strains of a song that has great meaning to me in Rochester's regard, but that I only hear on significant occasions, began to play and I stood with damp eyes and in awe and wonder holding his flowers as Rochester sent this gift to me. The only words I could appreciate before reaching the check-out point were:

When night has come and the land is dark
And the moon is the only light we'll see,
No, I won't be afraid, no I won't be afraid
Just as long as you stand by me.

Rochester has always stood by me.

Two years ago the following poem was given to me at Home Depot.

INFUSED

Today I will buy
    many plants
        to honor your life.
What will I spy
    along each
        row—
As I wander
    the aisles at
        Home Depot.

The outside section
    is alive with color
        and green bushes
           and trees.
I am at ease
    in this scene.
I walk in the breeze
    seeing flowers
        and whispering
           your name.
But I am not ready
    to choose
        from these hues.
I am infused
    with your presence.

For now—
    that is enough.

For my beloved   Jan
Rochester
on his birthday
May 30, 2005
written in Rochester, NH

MEDITATION FORTY-EIGHT

Jottings

Like the spontaneous jottings in a journal, sometimes in order and sometimes not, the following "Jottings" are thoughts that out of the blue came to me while writing and nearing completion on this book, yet they somehow did not seem to be meant for any specific meditation already completed or in progress. They are little sharings for you from my heart to add to the complete over-all picture of and gift of Ellis's and Rochester's lives in this, their book.

> *Like the memory of our loved ones, grief will never disappear,*
> *we just grow stronger to support the weight of it.*
>
> —George Anderson

A spontaneous jotting into my steno pad following a sudden overwhelming short period of intense grief.

AUGUST 6, 2004

If you have walked this earth and not loved at least one person or animal that when they passed it did not seem as if your very heart and soul was ripped from you and you walk as if it is you too who has passed—then you cannot understand the grief of another who has had this experience and that it is on-going and forever.

Many react differently but to those who are affected by a passing of a loved one in the way just described it can not be understood by those who do not grieve or who are not affected by a death be it for one such described or for anyone.

179

✸

A poem discovered in the same steno pad for the first time since I wrote it. Grief sometimes makes you overlook what you would normally never ignore.

WHISPERS

Every blade of grass
Not one the same
Speaks your name.

And as I pass
I see the leaves
They whisper to me
From the trees
As one who grieves.

For sweet Rochester   Jan
May 30, 2004

✸

Wishing Wells

A little planter hangs on the inside post of our screened-in-porch. It is a small round can painted dark green. Attached to it is a black trivet with white writing and two blue birds on either side, and a shiny yellow sun above the verse. The poem reads;

The kiss of the sun for pardon—
The song of the birds for mirth—
One is nearer God's heart in a garden
Than anywhere else on earth.

The planter was made years ago by my Dad and I keep a bunch of lovely life-like artificial violets in the can, symbolic of my Mother "Violet." Years ago I embroidered the same verse in a sampler and framed it as a gift for my Mother-in-law for her back screened-in-porch in Pennsylvania that overlooked her small garden. Later it was given to my daughter Laurel who hung it outside by her front door and her garden in Pennsylvania also. All of this embroidery of the little verse was inspired by my Dad's creating of the little trivet planter. A picture of this planter is seen in my book *Beneath The Stars and Trees.*

This was not the only planter he created but the only one with the trivet. One year my Mother dreamed of a project but needed my Dad's creativity to do it all. And he did it all! He completed an impressive display of wishing wells. They were just so sweet! He used coffee cans that he painted as he had my trivet planter, and then used his carpentry skills to design roofs for them all and a little handle on the side under each roof. When the handle was turned a tiny bucket he also created, was drawn up from the inside of the well on thin rope. These wishing wells were so amazing to me, especially seeing them all completed, dozens and dozens of them lined up on large tables in our basement where he had spent hours working on them. They were to be center pieces at a charitable function of a group that my Mother was active in. After the special dinner that was to raise money, the little wishing wells could also be bought to add money to the fund. For years a wishing well was in my parents' kitchen but after they went to Heaven I no longer know who it went to live with in our family. I wish it had been me.

🦋

Never will I forget my Dad; soft spoken, loving, and quiet but with a sense of humor that simply broke me up. Very especially as I grew older I appreciated his humor because it was subtle and unique, but as a child and teenager, I thought he was rather wonderful for all reasons. He was a precious *"Daddy"* to a little girl and I always think of him with such deep love. As a young man, I know he was quite handsome too (although he was always handsome to me). His inner being, his soul, made him so handsome and loving to me. He is deeply missed. I write poetry for him continuously.

🦋

Sleepwalking

In my childhood and early teen years I used to walk in my sleep. Late at night I would come down the stairs to the living room and roam around a bit until I was stopped. It was my Dad most of the time who corraled me gently for he was usually awake then. After using whatever method he chose, which I believe was just soft conversation so as not to startle me awake, he would then lead me back upstairs to my room. Another episode of my sleepwalking might not then occur for weeks or months. I never remembered what transpired but learned in the morning, and even in being told it did not help me to recollect.

I do not know if this is an unusual happening that goes from generation to generation, but it did occur with our son George. Like myself he sleepwalked and after all the children were in bed we would be downstairs in the den and hear someone coming down the stairs in either the living room or in the kitchen. The old home we lived in had a set of stairs to the kitchen area that we mainly used in preference to the front stairs. It was always a strange feeling to hear and see George approach from either direction totally in his own little world and we were not a part of it. Occasionally only he would talk but not saying anything relevant to what he was doing or why. He was not speaking to us, that was obvious. At times he would come down one set of stairs and circle through the rooms and go up the other set. It varied. And then he would go back to sleep in bed and I would do a final check on him. His sleepwalking was much more frequent and aggressive in nature than I was ever told mine was, and we often worried that he might go outside if we were not on the first floor when he appeared. Naturally doors were locked in winter but not in summer earlier in the evenings. We were just always cautious in his regard.

Eventually my parents installed a gate at the top of the stairs to keep me on the second floor but that had been some years after I began sleepwalking. That gate remained there in the years following my parents' passings and was there when several of our children lived there with their young children.

With that in mind some years after George began to sleepwalk, Bob installed a gate at the top of our front steps. There was already a door at the top of the back stairs. At times one or both obstacles would stop George, but usually they did not prove to be a barrier. He eventually stopped sleepwalking. As yet none of George's three young children sleepwalk. I often wonder if one or both of my parents may have done this. It was a part of my childhood I connect to my Dad.

🦋

Always With Me

I share in these *Jottings* a blessed incident, one of numerous similar ones since Rochester passed. What I write here of him gently touching me is something he lovingly did often in life. There is no doubt when it occurs now in spirit frequently. Too, the intense vibrational heat on my legs mentioned has been a gift to me since shortly after he passed, morning and night. It occurs every evening as I sit on the sofa with my legs stretched down a portion of its length and my back against the arm so I may read or watch TV. Rochester always laid on my legs and lap then all his life and continues to since he passed. This occurs in bed also. I have written this in my other books and enter it again to say it forever happens—a blessed gift.

This was a brief journal entry.

Incredible heat on my legs last night and during the night and in morning. I did not want to get up. The intensity is so much. Also I felt Rochester touch and caress the left side of my face near my eye and upper cheek. He did this so often with his soft little paw. It was amazing. I knew instantly it was him and talked to him as I always do. It continued for approximately four minutes. Thank you sweet Rochester.

I Know

Every day he is about—
Though some would say I am without.
A being is not always seen—
There is a moment so serene—
I know—I simply know—and then—
My loved one touches me again.
Like a feather-brush of air—
Telling me that he is there.

For beloved   Jan
Rochester   August 3, 2007

Only briefly mentioned earlier elsewhere in this book, I learned soon after my Dad passed away that our youngest daughter Janna was not only sad at home but softly crying at times in school and trying to go unnoticed. But the teacher shared this with me and she understood then why it was happening. This was Janna's first experience with grieving and she loved my Dad. She was eight years old and had lost her first grandparent and friend, the same age I was when I lost my grandmother, my Mother's mother, and the only grandparent I had ever known and loved. Janna, in time, became emotionally stronger. I do not remember how I responded over time to this impact to my life. In the same time frame our third oldest daughter Barbara entered Nursing School and had her capping ceremony at Roxborough Memorial Hospital a short period later, and we took my Mother to this ceremony hoping it would be emotionally helpful to her. It was one of the few times she allowed us into her life after my Dad's passing. She loved Barbara and was very proud of her as I know my Dad is.

Less than a year later in October 1978, our daughter Laurel had a beautiful wedding and reception, the planning of which began the end of the previous year. She knew my Dad could not be at her wedding but we did not know then that my Mother would be absent also. But we believe both were present that day in Spirit for both my Dad and Mother love Laurel so much.

✖

After receiving the Census Records from our son-in-law Rob regarding the Gray family history, Bob learned on-line that the name Gray is the 87th most popular family name in the United States. When I was growing up in Philadelphia and when living in the suburbs of that city after marriage, I never knew another Gray in all those years except my Uncle George in New Jersey. It simply was an unheard of name there. But here in New Hampshire and all of New England it is an extremely well-known and popular name. Our friend Mike Burnham in Rhode Island who has written many kind words for the covers of a number of my books, and is an author too, also has a grandparent in his family that is a Gray on his Mother's side from New Hampshire. We have compared family lineage after Rob sent me mine, but there is none the same. Nevertheless it was interesting to examine and compare the histories and there were a few names similar.

✖

Beloved Husband and Dad and Dog

Many, many books about grieving and afterlife have ministered to me in these past five years since Rochester passed. As I have written elsewhere, though I now have an enormous library just on these subjects alone, I know it will continue to grow. I do, however, truly appreciate and absorb these books through extensively attentive and multiple readings of most of the books. One exceptional book in this group has been referred to occasionally here in my book through several quotations from it, and that is Patti Davis's *The Long Goodbye*. Like another author appreciated, Geneen Roth, who wrote about her Dad and her cat that I have told you about, Patti Davis has written mainly about her Dad but with tender and sensitive words in a chapter also about the loss of her beloved dog Sadie. I have learned a long time ago I am not alone in experiencing the amazing and precious impact a beloved animal companion can have upon one's life while they are on earth and then eternally from Heaven.

Patti Davis not only writes so tenderly about her Dad sharing times together so similar as to moments and days I shared with my Dad—that one basically could not tell that one precious Dad was the President of the United States later in his life when he passed, or an unknown precious Dad in the City of Philadelphia. Too, she writes about her deeply loved dog, her faithful companion of ten years, and what Sadie means to her and her dying in her arms as Rochester did in mine. Sadie comes to her in dreams and teaches her about eternity and that death is not an ending. She feels her at the end of her bed as I have experienced Rochester walking and more. She believes Sadie to be waiting and that she is a gentle messenger, and too, that she will be waiting for her Dad to help him cross over. I read this chapter often and many other sections of her book concerning her Dad and then I begin it often and read it again from beginning to end. Though Rochester did not know my Dad on earth, her Sadie had been with her Dad just a few times.

I share these things with you not because of any political interests I have, for I am not of any definite political party and vote for the man not the party. I did respect President Reagan however for many reasons, both when I appreciated and enjoyed him as a movie star in my earlier years and then as President. I identify with his wife Nancy Reagan and her remarks also both in her daughter's book and in a very loving interview several months ago by Larry King. She told of her husband's incredible diaries that she had just had published and how he was so disciplined he wrote in his diary every night, and she showed one of the five large leather bound diaries that he had completed. He not only wrote presidential comments but every day ordinary accounts of his life. In reference to the time he was shot and almost killed he wrote simply that "it hurt." So childlike and sweet. And of this man who tried to assassinate him, he wrote that he had to forgive the man or he could not expect God to forgive him. Very powerful but simply said.

Nancy Reagan, so in love with her husband and he with her, stated that many say that it gets much easier as time passes. But she emphatically said, *"Not for me."* She feels spiritually connected to him as does his daughter, and she softly stated how it does not get better. She misses him more than ever, even more than in the beginning when he first passed. She wants reminders of him all around her in the house. All she and her daughter expressed are what I too try to express in my books. I experience grief in a comparable depth as do they, though it seems even more so. Yet who can measure degrees of pain and of grief? Only God. I have heard Patti Davis interviewed twice previously by Larry King also and identified so deeply with her in her sharings on grieving. Though they spoke of the former President of the United States, his wife was truly speaking of her "Ronnie" and his daughter of her "Dad." I speak of a Dad also and of a beloved animal companion. Nancy Reagan also spoke words I have thought and said as have so many others I have discovered in recent years who have lost both their parents. She states "You realize you are nobody's little girl anymore." There is a deep sadness realizing that truth no matter how old you are. But we change in many ways when this happens. More of our true and inner self gradually sometimes steps timidly forward, yet forever carries on the life and memories of our loved ones in Heaven. And they still live!

I share these writings and this interview in detail for perhaps in addition to this book you are reading and others of mine previously, you might find help in all that I have told you here and how it touches my life and gives a certain gentleness and peace.

֎

Being mindful in the morning sets you on a path to nourish your being through the hours that follow. All these years I have been slipping into my own places and spaces of prayer; a quiet corner, a back pew of a church before daily Mass, a wooden Adirondack chair on a wooden platform by the lake, and rooms of solace and aloneness, all nourishing the gentleness within me so it softly arises and overcomes any emotion that may be the opposite. Returning frequently to such a place is pure blessing. To spend each day writing in such an atmosphere of love and gentleness is pure gift. And for almost sixteen years a precious creature sent by God was the epitome of gentleness sharing this dear child-like room—a room of dreams, imagination, wonder, transformation, devotion, hope, forgiveness, compassion, and beauty. And always enchantment—and love eternal. And this precious creature's spirit will inhabit this place of gentleness as long as I inhabit it. And I grow in grace and gentleness.

GENTLENESS

Gentleness flows from a heart
    that has known the opposite.
It flows from a heart
    free of greed
      and the need
        to control
          or extol
            its own goodness.
Oft times Gentleness has lived
    through despair —
      and the care
      that it gives
        to those who are hesitant
        or fear
Is a precious restorative essence
    so spirit filled and dear
      that it can only be received
        and felt and drawn inward
        and believed
          and lived out
            for all days of one's life.

Jan
November 2004

Everything I wrote about in my four previous books in regard to the life we lived and that I continue to live with Rochester in spirit still remains the same. It is as if he *just passed*. It is as I hoped it would be and prayed for with all my heart.

All the dear remembrances shall always remain that I wrote of in *Corridors*. His flowered tin containing his ashes still accompanies me all about the cottage. Wherever I am, it is with me. It does not sit on a shelf. It is part of my life. I continuously have dreams, subtle contacts

and too, occasional appearances of him as well as his every night and morning presence through intense heat and static electric-like currents on my legs. I wear and always shall wear Rochester's red collar upon my left arm. I never remove it. And each evening after completing my day of writing I kneel down next to the bed in our writing room beside his fluffy wildlife quilt he loved to lie in the center of as I wrote, and I say prayers for us and talk to him about many things. Each Friday at 5 PM I still keep our Holy Hour, the Hour within which Rochester entered Heaven. The Hour is always extended, for I am lost in prayer and another world with him. To honor him, his water dish is always filled on his small maple table and several pieces of Iams are on a plate, a different plate of his each day. Iams was his "treat" not his basic food. Pennies arrive regularly for me from Heaven, and upon my arrival home from anywhere I still go to the bedroom where I know he has run ahead in spirit to wait and greet me on the side of the bed, even though he has also been with me on any outing. *Wherever I am—he is!* These are just a few of my never, ending *Holy Connections* with him. There are so many more. Always keep *Holy Connections* with your loved one. Your loved ones are with you. And write everything in your journal.

I can only conclude as I did in the previous books of mine and tell you that my grief is as fresh and overwhelming today as it was March 8, 2002, as I prayed it always would be. I know there are many others who also are as I am concerning their loved ones in spirit, be they human or animal. Too, I have been given *"The Gift of Tears"* that I prayed for, and this is a gift divine as I journey along this corridor. My tears flow every day for Rochester. I pray now as I did upon the completion of my previous four books that I may always have deep understanding for others in their grief, and try to help them even if from afar, yet never interfere. This book and all my books are my gifts to you, and Rochester and I pray they will fill you with love and consolation in your grieving and living and travelling your corridor.

portions from *A Pilgrim on Life's Road—*
Guidance for the Traveller—A Continuing Journey

In each of my books except the first, I have included a prayer written by Bob, and I will include it in this book also. He wrote it a number of years ago adapted from an old prayer we recited as children and his is far more comforting. This prayer is in addition to our own silent prayers at night and my blessing Rochester's forehead with the Sign of the Cross which I always did when he was in body and now do gently too in spirit. Perhaps you will want to pray this prayer as you travel this passage. It is assuring and childlike.

> As I lay down to sleep this night,
> Please keep me safe till morning light.
> Grant me sleep and needed rest,
> And fill my dreams with happiness.
> For Lord I know that with you near,
> There's nothing that I have to fear.
> Guide me where you want to lead,
> And be with those I love and need.

Before Rochester passed, Bob had also written music for this prayer and recorded it on his electronic keyboard on a separate tape. It is beautiful.

Before settling down for prayer and sleep upon my legs, Rochester often climbed gently up the front of me as I sat in a half-reclining position and he would push his little forehead against mine numerous times, a form of kiss. Often he would gently pat my cheek with his soft white marshmallow paw, a tender touch of his love—not only at night but often in our writing room when he was on my lap or desk. I share now the music of the poem prayer.

As I Lay Down To Sleep

Robert A. Kolb Jr.

Solace of Creativity

On a metaphysical level—when she knits for someone she loves,
she thinks of that person continually throughout the project and knows
that there is an intangible quality to the finished garment
that the person will somehow feel.

—Bernadette Murphy

Because she is very creative and is a very good knitter—
she has a job in a yarn store in the business district of our community.
It is about a 15-minute walk or so from our home.
She not only sells yarn to customers, but she is giving knitting instructions
and gets extra pay for the teaching. This is important work for the war effort
because women are encouraged to knit clothing for our fighting men
and boys overseas and for all of the brave servicemen
no matter where they are sent and stationed.

—from *Silent Violence*

My Mother had a generous and giving heart and nature, always reaching out to others. The opening paragraph tells too in the writing of her little daughter, of some of the work she was interested in doing. During the second world war she worked extensively for the Red Cross knitting scarves, hats, long helmets and gloves for our boys in the service. So many articles were knitted in both khaki wool and navy blue. She headed up such a group, and women came to our home often to pick up the yarn and other supplies to knit these necessities and then to return the finished items. My Mother in turn returned them to the Red Cross for shipment overseas and elsewhere. I am proud to say as a little girl I too knitted some of these necessities with the guidance from my Mother as she worked on her own knitting. My Dad would frequently deliver some of the finished knitted items to other destinations I was never aware of so they could begin their long journey overseas. I was proud of all the work my Mother was doing for the war effort and that my Dad showed interest and helped her. My Dad loved to see the two of us together like this and happy and laughing. He called us "his girls."

From the knitting of my first khaki scarf in the garter stitch I enjoyed the art of knitting and I went on to make other scarves and have knitted all of my life as a result, sometimes in more intensity and interest and often with periods of no knitting at all.

Now in these past years my writing comes first, but there is also occasional knitting and it is always meaningful to me to do. My daughters I taught as they were growing up and they knit with enjoyment, and many of my granddaughters also knit beautifully. I am the recipient of numerous lovely scarves created in various styles, designs and color made by daughters and a granddaughter. They knit gifts for others and too, knit for themselves.

After my Dad passed away and my Mother was involved in the aftermath of my Dad's and Uncle's passings and business related matters, as well as limited time in her costume jewelry store, she was more withdrawn from us. She was deeply grieving as I have related earlier and never ceased grieving until her passing. After her entrance into Heaven and we eventually had to go through things in her home, we found enormous treasure in the little upstairs middle room den of their row home at 6231. There were two recliners in that room and a little television that they enjoyed together and some books. There behind the recliners that had sat side by side with a lamp between them, were piles and piles of knitted and crocheted scarves and shawls. Not known to us then my Mother had obviously sat night after night knitting and crocheting beautiful items of every hue. Knitting and crocheting or any handwork can be such a comfort and release and she passed her nightly hours without the physical presence of my Dad creating such exceptional keepsakes. Such love and tears went into each one.

It gave me great joy to gradually distribute the items to family members and her close friends praying for guidance before I gave each one away.She left no note as to whom they were to be given. Every recipient was so appreciative.

It was not until I was in the very midst of writing these memories now about her knitting and crocheting to help her survive in her grief that I remembered that I had done a similar thing but am only now seeing it as such.

Following my Dad's passing four months after , even though I had not crocheted in some time and needed to be re-taught, I began to crochet a very large bed size afghan in the beginning of 1978. I did not know my Mother was crocheting and knitting her heart out through her hands and needles and yarn to help herself. When I finished the first afghan, and it was very beautiful and big, I began another. And another! And another! My Mother passed then in September 1978 and by November I had made seven of these large afghans, each in a combination of three to four complimentary colors and each afghan totally different. I had crocheted for nine months and had continued crocheting nightly after my Mother's passing while caring for my family and too, weekly attending a meeting with my Priest friend in preparation for entering my new church in December. I had made the afghans for several of my children for different significant reasons, and Bob, and for others. The one for Bob was carelessly packed with belongings in our permanent move to New Hampshire and left in the storage area with them for numerous years. We did not have room in this small cottage for these belongings. In searching for something late last Fall in this storage area that I never intrude upon, I found Bob's afghan totally exposed, not in a wrapping or carton. I was shocked, and not one little moth or mouse had buried into it! A rush of memories flooded over me of that era. I had just begun to write this book. I rescued the afghan and washed it and it is so beautiful in colors of dark brown, very pale yellow, peach and orange, colors appropriate for our past den in Jenkintown, though I should have made it in shades of green—Bob's favorite color. The afghan is perfect and just like new, so bright and colorful! A long ago treasure found. Normally my Mother and I would have discussed and shared our creative activities, but grieving changes people. We are never the same. We are different.

And we are also often "into ourselves" in ways difficult to describe. Neither of us knew we were endlessly creating while lost in memories of Dad, and that I was compelled to continue creating after her passing too. I will always connect these intense periods of creating mainly with my Dad but also with the Mother who taught me to knit and crochet. Though she enjoyed other handcrafts that I then inspired her to learn, and that we created with equal fervor, the yarn and the needles are symbolic of Dad.

Though there were other instances of compulsive handwork before and after Dad's passing, none compared to my Mother's scarves and my afghans. But as a teenager I also enjoyed knitting endless pairs of colorful argyle socks and too after the passing of my Dad in August I knitted six scarves in time to give as Christmas gifts to a very special group of friends in Massachusetts (who were regularly in New Hampshire as we were), before the crocheting of the afghans began in January 1978. In a sense even the socks were connected to Dad for he always enjoyed seeing me

Photos of three afghans I made back in 1978 (there were seven total, but these belong to Laurel, Barbara and Bob).

knit and made humorous but encouraging comments as I worked away with all the little spindles dangling from my work. It seems as if while lost in memories my Mother and I also could have been unknowingly trying to knit and crochet Dad's being and essence even more deeply into ours.

And though I did not knit after the passing of Rochester with the exception of two scarves in more recent years, I began to write a book about him and our life together two days after he passed. And then, like my afghans, another book on the solace of solitude, another concerning travelling as a pilgrim on this journey and still yet another of poetry and precious things related, and now this book of Ellis's and Rochester's. Do you see? Seven afghans after Dad passed and now five books after Rochester's passing. There is probably a label for someone with my behavior, one possibly described as obsessive, but it all derives its source from loving so deeply and forever and ever and ever.

Knitting and crocheting are transforming to one's spirit. They take you on an inner journey. Perhaps my Mother felt an internal peace to some degree. These handcrafts help to express love for others as you go to "another place," and things around you become less intense and soften as you meditate and your hands create. I know this truth. It is also a therapy to quiet a turbulent mind for it is soothing and calming. Again, I know this to be true. For myself it can at times be similar to a Rosary for it is centering and spiritual as you finger the yarn, just as you lovingly and gently move your fingers over the beads and pray, and enter into another deeper reality.

When knit by someone who loves and cares, be it for a person the knitter knows or does not know, the recipient is being embraced in care and prayer.

—Jan

Many faiths see, in the human desire to create, a reflection of the divine creative spark. Some might say that when we create, when we tap into the wellspring of beauty and aesthetic harmony that surrounds us, we are most in tune with God.

—Bernadette Murphy from *Zen and The Art of Knitting*

Peace in the Woods

Come with me to the enchanted forest.
Trust the magic in the air; it is real.
Take it with you wherever you go,
for the magic you feel and want
is yours if you simply believe.

—Melody Beattie from *Journey to the Heart*
(as in *Beneath the Stars and Trees*)—by Jan

VISITING NEW HAMPSHIRE

The sun is shining brightly,
The birds are chirping lightly—
Branches softly sway, as breezes
    pass, throughout the day.

The air is warm and mild,
Awakening each sense—
Providing peace and pleasure,
Instead of feeling tense.

The lake is blue and still—
Lapping gently on the sand—
Its beauty can be seen and heard,
When on surrounding land.

A place that's so serene,
And wonderful to be—
A place alive with green,
Brings happiness to me.

—Barbara Jan Frances Egan
July 1, 2002

Written in a previous meditation in this book I relate about my arrival in New Hampshire from Pennsylvania following the passing of my Dad the previous week. Climbing onto my prayer chair platform and sitting in the chair overlooking the lake, I finally was able to find release, and tears just flowed and flowed. We did not yet live permanently here in the woods and I could only be here a short period with our family.

Following the passing of Rochester, our daughter Barbara came from Jenkintown on one of her special visits to be with us in June 2002. She spent twelve days in the last weeks of June. As I have written in *Corridors*, just as I have been writing poems as gifts to Rochester, Barbara gave me both the gift of her presence to lighten my heart, and a poem. On Sunday night June 30th as she sat in the striped rocking chair in front of the stairs opposite me on the sofa, Rochester appeared behind her coming down the steps. It was only a brief moment that I saw him there slightly above Barbie, then he disappeared. My heart pounded but I said nothing. I was overjoyed! Later before she left New Hampshire I would tell her, and she both questioned and then accepted.

On July 1st before she left she sat in her same chair overlooking the gardens and lake and wrote a poem. It is so meaningful to me that I wish to include it here in this book also as I did in *Corridors*. It speaks of the peace and serenity of life here that is ours, and that she also has experienced here since she was a young girl, and that Rochester has always known and loves and shares forever with us. It was that peace I found here also following the passing of my Dad, and like Barbie then in 2002 I could only be here that summer in 1977 less than two weeks.

At Thanksgiving in 1977 we returned and we brought my Mother here too to the snowy woods to experience a brief period by the frozen lake in her deep grief. She came bearing not only her love and grief but a small packet of photos of my Dad that gave her consolation. That packet of pictures is now mine. She also knitted as a release all the while she was here and was blessed by incredibly beautiful sunsets.

The poem that opens this meditation is the poem written by Barb. It holds so much meaning and love. When she returned to Jenkintown in July, within days one of her and husband Frank's beloved cat companions also entered Heaven, dear Gus. Though a sweet black and white cat with a boy's name who too had visited New Hampshire with Barbie and us in 1985, she was a little girl. It was a sad time in 2002.

While nearing completion on this book our daughter Janna and husband Bill and their three children Dahlia, Rebecca and Nicholas (also known as Cole) visited us to vacation. Janna and Bill had been married here by the lake in 1994 which shows the extent of their love for this lovely place in the woods. Janna had been vacationing here since she was a little girl of eight years (like their Rebecca is now) and following the passing of my Dad and her Pop-Pop.

Photo of Cole, standing in a hole he dug by the lake the summer he was here following the writing of his poem (2007).

In the mail before their arrival here last week we received a poem written by nine year old Cole in school shortly before summer vacation began. His teacher was most impressed with it and it is a "keeper" to us. Again it speaks of the consolation a certain place can bring to individuals. We and Rochester and many others in this family and even those not related, have continued to find this peace and consolation here on *"Higher Ground"* in this enchanted forest.

I leave now also on these pages Cole's poem with his Aunt Barbara's. Though perhaps not intended, it was written on his mother Janna's and Rochester's birthday, my Janna who helped to bring my Rochester into my life.

GRANDMOM AND GRANDPOP'S WOODS

Up north,
In New Hampshire,
My favorite vacation spot,
I'm so relaxed,
I fall asleep,
Then the sun,
Warms me awake,
There are animals everywhere,
Popping out like daisies,
The trees are a sea of green.
I see the lake,
From my chair,
On the beach,
With the waves curling.
New Hampshire,
My favorite vacation spot.

by Cole VanDorick
May 30, 2007

This quotation below speaks of our home in the woods. The quotation that opens this meditation and the following one appear in the very beginning of my book *Beneath The Stars and Trees* to give the readers an inkling of what it is like to live here even before they read the book that tells each detail of that deep joy.

Sometimes a man hits upon a place to which he mysteriously feels that he belongs. Here is the home he sought, and he will settle amid scenes that he has never seen before, among men he has never known, as though they were familiar to him from his birth. Here at last he finds rest.

—W. Somerset Maugham from *The Moon and Sixpence*
as in *Beneath the Stars and Trees*

June 2, 2007—Happy Day!

Happy Birthday dear Dad! I have been thinking of you all through the day and now as the sun begins to set upon the lake, I leave this poem upon the page as a little gift. At approximately 5 PM as I sat with pencil and paper earlier writing this book, this poem just poured forth from within , interrupting my other writing as I attempted to capture it. It all occurred in ten minutes. Happy Birthday, Dad!

HEAVENLY BIRTHDAY

Dad, it is your birthday today!
Yes, yours—Ellis George Gray!
In Heaven do they celebrate
your date?
Is there a warm plate
filled with mashed potatoes
pot roast, corn and sliced tomatoes?
Did Mother bake
her delicious white cake
with chocolate icing?
Is she busy slicing
it with care?
O such fare!
Are Rochester and Mitzi
there with you?
Perhaps some vanilla ice cream
for them too.

I see you all in my mind's eye —
And embrace each one.—You did not die!

For Dad   Janny
on his birthday
June 2, 2007
with great love

My Dad (Ellis) and me
(He is 31 years and I am 1½ years.)

MEDITATION FIFTY-TWO

Mary

MARY'S ROSARY

On the chain the beads abound—
They circle 'round—and there is found,
A peace of heart in those who pray—
Our Blessed Mother's Beads each day.

The Rosary softly slips through fingers—
While on our souls her presence lingers.
As we lift daily our intentions,
She removes our apprehensions.

In moments still—this Chain of Love—
Links us to Mystical Rose above.
And as we pray the precious Beads—
Dear sweet Mary intercedes.

—Jan

I have at times mentioned Mary and the Rosary in this book as I have in previous ones. When I began to pray the Rosary for my Dad in 1977, I believe Mary was drawing me closer. Though I was Protestant she and the Rosary were strengthening from that point on through the years. Because she is so loving and wise, she knew I would need her more than ever when March 8th arrived in 2002 when Rochester passed and so she gently drew me even more close. And that is what I want to share this day as I have previously in *Corridors* and other books, for perhaps there are others who have kept Mary at a safe distance and refuse to allow her near, and maybe hearing how she has comforted me so many many times in ordinary days and nights but too in deep sadness and turmoil of heart, she may be allowed to comfort you also.

You do not have to be a Catholic or Protestant or any religion—you simply have to need consoling, comfort, and understanding, and love, and she will come to you. You do not even need a Rosary, for that is asking a lot of someone who may never have ever been near a Rosary before. I have just needed to share with you how Mary gradually entered my life since 1977. And all through the years Rochester was with me in earthly form she was part of our life and much more so since he entered Heaven. Having no earthly Mother for many years, or Dad, and feeling often like an orphan, it has helped me so very much to feel deeply Mary's love in a more apparent way. Her presence is here and comforting me as I live in this new dimension with my dear little Rochester—and too, because of Rochester, with my Dad and other loved ones. I chose the name of "Mary" as my confirmation name to honor her the night of December 13th, 1978 when I became Catholic. I know so many personally who are comforted by Mary and too by praying the Rosary, whether praying it in traditional form or in ways thay have been personally led to pray. Not all are Catholic. As I have written in a previous book, beads are used in prayer by those of many faiths and even those not in one particular faith.

One who has helped me along this corridor these past five years in various ways is John Edward. He lost his Mother at a much earlier age than I lost my parents. The Rosary has been prayed by him multiple imes daily for many years and for precious reasons that can be read about in his books. He has said and written many deeply spiritual words but this quotation is one said simply so that others may consider the Rosary for themselves.

> As many others who pray the Rosary have discovered, having one can be like carrying a cell phone that connects us directly to Heaven—and that's a call you always want to make.
>
> —John Edward from *Practical Praying*
> *Using the Rosary to Enhance Life*

I do not ever carry a cell phone—but I always have a Rosary with me. It is made up of many spiritual "*links*" to Jesus, Mary and Rochester and to Dad and other loved ones.

When I was praying the Rosary Rochester would often pat it gently, sometimes holding it secure in his paw and at those times I was so moved by this I just sat in prayer quietly with him and waited until he released it. It is no wonder the Rosary has become a Holy link between Rochester and myself connecting us now in spirit.

> *It is written and said by my spiritual friend John Edward that when we pray the Rosary for our loved ones in Heaven it is heard as musical notes by them drawing them closer and closer to us. The Rosary or other prayers of repetition of all faiths are music to their ears reminding them again and again of our deep love for them. You cannot imagine what those words meant to me when I firsst read them shortly after the passing of Rochester. We had been praying the Rosary for years together and now it would continue to be a heavenly cord for us. And so I pray the Rosary in an extremely personal way numerous times daily.*
>
> —Jan

Though many pray the Rosary in groups, it still remains for me a very personal and individual prayer and is one I only do when alone with Rochester, previously, when in body and now in spirit. Meditation and contemplation too are part of my daily prayers. I cannot emphasize enough how these prayer forms will comfort and bring solace and connections to those who grieve—as well as to those who do not.

MEDITATION FIFTY-THREE

A Glimpse

A thing of beauty is a joy forever.
Its loveliness increases; it will never
Pass into nothingness;

—John Keats, *A Thing of Beauty*

In a poetry book for children that I buy for a grandchild in December 2004, there are several poems in it I take time to copy into my journal for my own continued reading. One in particular touches me so deeply. The poet, Janet S. Wong, writes that her mother says the spirits of the dead visit in dreams.She gives instructions in her sixteen lines of poetry as to what you must do if you are chosen by a loved one, how your must pull all the air around you gulping it and swallowing it down, and if you do those memories will stick like cotton candy. This poem appears in *Night Garden—Poems from the World of Dreams*. It appears too in my journal and often in my memory. Therefore seven months later when I have a visit from my own two beloved spirits, this poem again brings comfort as it surfaces often in my mind. This is my incomparable visitation.

In July of 2005, I have a dream or vision, I do not know which, so vivid it is with me now still in August of 2007. Though it is written first in my steno pad by the side of my bed shortly after experiencing it, I record it in my journal also. But because it is engraved within my heart I will forever remember it in other dimensional ways aside from my continual trust in the importance of writing.

In this vision I see my Dad and Rochester in back view walking together away from me, side by side. It is so sweet to me, so tender. Rochester is on my Dad's right. There are no surroundings that I can remember, no roads, no grass or trees, just my two loved ones. It is only the two of them closely side by side walking, walking, but not talking. Two silent ones who cannot speak to each other while on earth or to me or to anyone in the normal way of speech, yet I know in ways not explainable their deep love for me and now for each other. This vision is so utterly precious, for it is given to me to confirm that my Dad is taking care of Chester just as I begged him to do the night Chester passed. I believe too, they are indicating I am to follow them in spirit and one day my journey will take me to them and our reunion in Heaven. It is a vision I see again and again in spirit ever since that night, especially when I am having a sad or difficult period. Thank you dear ones, for allowing me this glimpse beyond the veil to carry until I too am walking with you. It truly sticks within me like cotton candy.

Afterword

In the privacy of my own home, I grieve and remember, like everyone else.
Applying a sense of poetry and my discipline as a writer
to those overwhelming feelings was tremendously useful to me.

—Roseanne Cash on the death of her parents
from *Always Too Soon*

It is time now to come to an ending of this book written for and about Ellis and Rochester. But the thoughts and remembrances of them and the great love for them and the contacts from them shall be forevermore, and until we are reunited in Heaven. They are endearing treasured beings that lead and guide and watch over me for all time. Our mutual love is overwhelming and eternal. That I was able to write all that I did about my Dad is truly amazing for I did not know all the many things written in these pages before I began. The more I continued to write the more I was given. I know now without question that I was meant to write this book and that I was led to do it and helped by my Dad and Rochester. I could write endlessly about Rochester for we shared every moment of our lives and still do, but all that is written in these pages, I believe is all that is meant to be at this particular time. Ellis's and Rochester's special book has come to an end and I pray it will bless all who read it. May it show too that books do not only have to be limited in content to extraordinary people or animals. It is often those quiet and unassuming individuals or creatures lives that speak just as deeply to the hearts of those who read. Their lives and how they lived are precious in the sight of God just as are the wonderful heroes and the well-known, be they animal or human.

God loves us all. And I truly love these two dear sweet guys that bless my life and always have and shall.

I include the opening quotatin for it speaks of myself and it is as if I am saying the words. This woman's father, Johnny Cash, has always had great spiritual impact on me through his singing and words and I have written of him in a previous book.

Perhaps you will begin to write in a journal if you are not doing so now and capture thoughts that crossed your mind as you read. Too perhaps you will begin to write more about your own life and the special people or animals that have blessed it along your passage. Always write. It is a blessing beyond explanation that you will discover once you begin.

I add one thing, a correction, to the pages and that is a discovery of incorrect dates. Because of the wonderful surprise of receiving the family history of dates from the Census Bureau from our son-in-law Rob as I wrote of in the Introduction, we learned the correct ages of my Uncle George and Uncle Raymond, brothers of my Dad. They were all seven years apart, my Dad the oldest born in 1904. George then was born in 1918 and Raymond in 1911. These correct dates make George two years younger than the date that appears on his Memorial Card in *Meditation 12—Ellis, George and Mysteries*. Either George's daughter put down the only correct date she knew or perhaps George's wife was older than he and they changed the date years before. Apparently in those days it seemed more necessary for the man to be older than his wife. George therefore was 77 when he passed away, not 79. I wanted to record the Memorial Card just as it was in that chapter. This was the situation with my Dad and Mother and is the reason I suggest it as a possibility for George and Marge. I did not know my Mother's true age until she passed and learned from papers she was a year and a half older than Dad. Since she was so obviously self-conscious about it we never had her date put on her gravestone out of love for her. It is not disrespectful to include it here for there are no longer any relatives or friends living on earth except our children. There was at the time we had the tombstone engraved in 1978.

I pray once read, you will pick this little book up again often to re-meet with Ellis and Rochester and to let your heart be touched anew by two gentle men of God. I will continue to follow them in spirit until I am walking with them in Heaven. And I believe then in our reunion and for all eternity I will hear their loving *audible* words.

Not everything on earth has a cure. There is no cure for loss, and no perfect mending of a broken heart. Life will not be normal again; normal is a word that passes on with our loved ones.

—George Anderson, *Walking in the Garden of Souls*

A Remembrance

"ROCHESTER"
T. PETERSON 7/03

Life-like 5x7 portrait of Rochester created by artist Tom Peterson, a gift from Tom and Sue Peterson from Colorado that arrived the very day that Rochester's book *In Corridors of Eternal Time* was finalized. It appears also in *Solace of Solitude, A Pilgrim on Life's Road* and *Cherishing*. This portrait has been drawn by a loving man I have never met and came to me in a handsome frame. How precious my friends have created such a gift for me. It indicates too the power of love and inspiration my Rochester causes to emanate to others. Tom and Sue have many beloved animal companions of their own and extend help to other animals in many ways. Rochester introduced us through Sue's reading of my *Journal of Love*.

EVER THERE

When the setting sun settles down on the tree tops
And pink and purple clouds float in the orange sky—
That is when my breath stops
For I know you did not die.
In this celestial beauty you come to me
And in the reflections upon the lake —
I stand in awe at all I see
And in our oneness illuminated in its wake.

In my soul you are ever there —
Yet I see you everywhere.

For my   Jan
sweet Rochester   August 10, 2007

ELLIS

A gentleman and no stranger
To the complexities of living —
He was a kind and loving father —
Protecting and self-giving.

I will always remember his humor —
His smile—and fun-loving ways —
His imprint upon his little girl
Remains for all her days.

For Dad   Janny
May 24, 2007
with love

Pictures for the Heart

This picture of Dad belonged to my Mother and was stuck in the lower corner of a small gold frame holding an instamatic photo. This instamatic photo too was of my Dad in the more recent years before his passing. This earlier photo is only about an inch square and there is no hint to where it had been taken. With the thoughtful expression on his face and his full head of hair we estimate him to be in his mid-thirties though we vacillate at times and have considered him to be in his early forties. Nothing was ever written on the back of any photos that became mine. This particular one I do cherish.

The sweet picture of Rochester below, and that is on a page in the front of this book beneath a picture of my Dad, is one that is so endearing to me. He is gazing upward with his beautiful golden eyes while lying on the back of our sofa. the sofa is in front of our sliding glass doors that allow a lovely view of flowers, rocks, green grass, trees and lake.

There is a deep significance to this picture for this sofa is like a bridge between two eras, or two worlds. He loved to be here and too, enjoy the squirrels and birds.

The beige sofa beneath the colorful slip cover over it belonged to my parents. Many times my Dad was seated there in my presence. The night he had been attacked and robbed it was on this sofa he was sitting when we arrived to pray with him. The sofa became ours a short while after they both passed away, and having little furniture in our rustic cottage we brought the sofa to New Hampshire.

In June 1986 after Rochester entered my life—he enjoyed lying on the back of my parents sofa. Though Dad and Rochester never met in this world, they did share the same sofa that sat in each of their homes. It truly was like a bridge between two worlds. That sofa is gone now, but they are alive together in Heaven forever.

Last night,
I spoke your name to the wind,
which told the trees,
which touched the sky,
which shone with moonlight
which filled my world
with dreams of you.

—Unknown

Laurel Elizabeth Kuhl and her little dog Layla.
Laurel was born on her Grandfather Ellis's birthday.

George Robert Kolb.
George is named after his Grandfather Ellis George.

Robert Ellis Hudson.
Bob's middle name is for his
Grandfather Ellis

My mother is the grand-daughter of Ellis George Gray. I am the fifth-born and third son of Ellis' oldest granddaughter, June; therefore, I'm thankful that my parents had such a great name left to name me: Robert Ellis Hudson. I am named after my two great-grandfathers, not to mention all the other wonderful Roberts who are in my family on both my mother's and father's side. There was only ONE Ellis, however, and I'm grateful to be able to carry that name on.

I know that my great-grandfather, Ellis George, was an engineer and a wonderful, committed father, grandfather, and Christian. He passed away thirteen years before I was born, so I never was able to meet him, but the knowledge that I am named after him is an honor, and gives me an extra measure of confidence to pursue my career as an engineer, like my father, grandfather, and great-grandfathers before me.

I am thankful for the life that Ellis George lived, for the father that he was to my grandmother and the grandfather he was to my mother, who lived with him for a time while my grandfather Kolb was overseas in the Navy. The legacy my great-grandfather Ellis Gray left helps to give me a foundation for my life and for my future. I'm proud to be named after such an incredible man.

Through the writing of this book that my grandmother is writing, I know I will come to know more about the man he was and what that can mean to me and my family. Thank you, Grandmom!

Robert Ellis Hudson

*6231 sign from Third Street in Philadelphia that hangs over our
cottage door that formerly spent years on Ellis' row home
in Philadelphia.*

Picture of 6231 N. Third Street, Philadelphia, Pennsylvania

*The side wall of the end home on Third St. (I lived the third home
from the corner), where the large gray air raid box sat that we young girls
sat upon. The dark marks on the stone wall at the bottom
indicate where the box sat and the length. The marks remain
after all these years. I visited and took this photo in November 2007*

*2043 Sunset Cliffs Blvd., San Diego, California
Our first apartment after we married and went to San Diego.
The windows of our apartment were the upper left. This photo was just
taken in 2007 by a good friend, Jim Wilson, who lives in San Diego and
was in the Navy at the same time with Bob. His kindness is such a gift.
The building looks exactly as it did in 1955. Exactly!!*

Ellis George Gray, 31 years

Dad (Ellis) with our daughter (his granddaughter), Barbara Jan (third child), 3 years

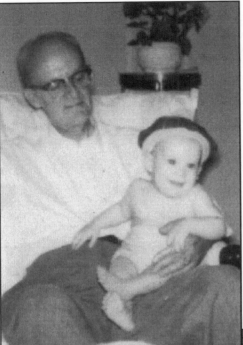

Dad (Ellis) and George Robert Kolb (Ellis' grandson and our son), taken on my Dad Ellis' 58th birthday, June 2, 1962. George was 6 months. George is named for my Dad's middle name.

My Dad Ellis with our youngest child—tiny daughter Janna Rebecca

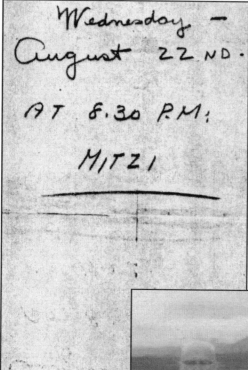

Actual photo of the treasured small paper I own (in Dad's printing), signifying Mitzi's death, that my Dad carried in his notebook for twenty-one years until his own passing.

Dad (Ellis) and my Uncle Elmer McKay (my mother's brother) on a vacation in Alaska (Mother took the picture).

The piano that I played as a child and teen years.
My Mother also played this piano. Since she went to Heaven,
it has been in our daughter Barbara's home. Barbara plays beautifully.

An earlier picture of my Dad seated at this piano in 6231.

Rochester
The collar he is wearing I wear on my arm
covered in black star-studded material

Ellis' six grandchildren (and our six children)
Top row: June Leslie, George Robert, Barbara Jan
Bottom row: Jessica Mae, Janna Rebecca, Laurel Elizabeth

Poems from the Heart

*In the essentials of what they meant to us, the dead live on with us
as long as we ourselves live. Sometimes we can speak to them
more readily than with the living.
I need no weapon against death because there is no death.
What does exist is the fear of death. That can be cured.*

—Herman Hesse, *Reflections*

WHOOSH

Poems are everywhere.
They hide out in grass
and flower petals—
in dirt and soft leaves—
by rippling lakes
and under rocks.
They hide behind bushes
and snuggle in
tree trunks
and long to be
caught and
expressed.
Yet
in their shyness
they hide away.
They are afraid
of the coldness

of eyes who
may misinterpret
their intentions
and beauty.
They want to
gently slip into
souls and heal
with their words.
The signal moment must
be the only one
meant for that
poem to come
to life.
And then you
will feel its
birth.
Whoosh—

Jan
May 24, 2005

I pray the poems that follow will gently slip into souls and heal and that you will feel their birth. Whoosh—

"YOUR HARRYSHIP"

A little gentleman is he—
So noble—and with dignity.
Faithful, quiet, contemplative—
A heart so filled with love to give.

Golden eyes glow with affection
Marmalade and white complexion.
A new love name has come to mind—
"Your Harryship"—so gentle, kind.

For one who's loved has love names known—
Not just the birth name that's his own.

Dedicated to   Jan
Rochester HARRY Whittier Kolb   February 14, 1993
("Your Harryship" love name
given by Bob—)

To clarify the name "Harry"—it is the *love name* given to Rochester by Bob. Not one that conforms, he has never called him his given name of Rochester or Chester. Bob has even occasionally referred to him as "Your Harryship" and inspired the above poem.

SETTLING IN

Little furry face and head—
An inch from mine—I lie in bed—.
He stares into my eyes and purrs
Then walks my body—he prefers—
To settle down on legs awhile,
Then moves to tummy—he knows I'll—
Not move an inch—he's here to stay
Because he knows now that we'll pray—,
I with my Rosary;—now the beads—
Know too, sweet paws and purrs and kneads.
In union with the breaths I take—
He's lulled to sleep until we wake.

Dedicated to   Jan
Rochester Harry Whittier Kolb   December 16, 1991

THE MARK OF A MAN

Another birthday without you
What's a saddened heart to do?
So many years we could have had.
Why did you go?—I miss you, Dad.

I often smile and think about—
A little quirk that caused you doubt—
And made you feel a lesser man,
Afraid again someone would pan—
The fact you had two permanent marks
Foolishly acquired on boyhood larks.

And so you never wore short sleeves—
Afraid that somehow you'd displease—
Your friends or family with your arms
As if tattoos should cause alarms!
A cherub babe and little star
One on each arm—they couldn't mar—
The man you were—the man you are.
(So insignificant—by far!)

You were a giant—yet felt small—
But in my eyes you stood so tall.
O Dad,—I very plainly see—
That I'm like you characteristically.
You chose long sleeves to cover you—!
A whole brown bag over me wouldn't do!

There were no tattoos on your soul—
On mine—may irregularities not take toll.
Aren't we crazy and quite vain—
To think our outer selves explain—
When actually Dad,—within each heart
It's there—that is the better part!

Dedicated to my Dad, Ellis George Gray,   Jan
on his 87th Birthday, June 2, 1991   June 2, 1991
(Died August 21, 1977)

WE JOURNEY ON

My cheeks wet with memory
    I walk the paths you once walked
      and where we talked
        throughout our home.
          I roam
            within
              as you
                still do.

    Up the stair
      each day I go—
    But then you know
      for you are there.

    And I write
      while you inspire—
    To set my thinking
      all afire—

    There in our room
      of joy and tears—
    Where we daily
      spend our years.

    Yes,—we journey on
      from day to day—
    On our eternal
      passageway.

For beloved Rochester   Jan
in the month   May 15, 2005
of his birthday—
May 30, 2005

THE INVITATION

This Father's Day—mysteriously part of my Father's spirit
Now lives in an old Inn.
His and my Mother's wished to endear it—
And establish spiritual residence again with kin.
They left their city home of life long years—
More recently shared with Granddaughter and her spouse—
And moved with them—sharing also farewell tears—
To this old New Hampshire house.

For many summers my parents had vacationed
On Lake Winnepesaukee;—there they had stationed
Themselves in peace and joy and sun.
Now returned to this state—a mystical conclusion has been spun.

Dedicated to Jessica who inspired this poem   Jan
when she said she had invited her   June 19, 1994
Grandparents to move with them to the Inn

HAPPY BIRTHDAY, DEAR DAD

You're eighty-nine, Dear Dad—it's true
And yet in Heaven your life is new—
And I shall never see you age—
No, never have that normal gauge—
And so envision you in ways—
We shared our lives in earlier days.

One thing I know—beyond that door—
You're just as handsome as before!
You're fun and witty—and still charming.
Do the angels find you quite disarming?

Dedicated to my Dad   Jan
Ellis George Gray
on his birthday, June 2, 1993

THIS PLACE

This place
        is a container of memories
            seemingly held
                in Heavenly light.
   It has been a Holy site
      to honor
          to leave offerings of love.
             God chose it
                  for our glorious meeting.

Today I leave again
       with great emotion
          and precious greeting—
             a shiny penny
                hidden quite well.
For you send me, dear one—
      with great devotion—
         a stream of pennies
           from Heaven.

For Beloved Rochester   Jan
written at the site   March 8, 2006
in Rochester, NH where
I adopted him.

Fourteen Years

Fourteen years ago he died—.
O how his life has signified—
Quietness and perseverance,
Love, support;—not interference.
He slipped away so silently—
Just how he lived;—compliantly.

It seems with every passing year
He's more alive and ever near!
Memories reign, remain—sustain—
And in my heart is his domain.

Dedicated to
my father—
Ellis George Gray
Died August 21, 1977
(14th anniversary)

Jan
August 20, 1991

Gray

I have decided to take my Father's last name.
Always I have worn it in my heart—and hidden—,
And now there is this need to be one and the same—
As if mysteriously called to it;—and bidden.

His name could not be carried on by a son.
Having only a daughter—I am the one
That must see that it is carried.
And I shall do that now—though I am married.

Dropping two middle names into my inner being—
Will spiritually signify that I am agreeing—
To raise up then his name given to me at birth;
To bring it forth anew—and show its worth.

Those middle names are no more lost than was his name.
   Within my heart they'll replace his—that I reclaim.

Dedicated to Bob   Jan
who encouraged this change—   June 20, 1994
officially made June 2, 1994
on my Dad's 90th birthday

THE INTERIOR CELEBRATION

Another birthday's come, dear Dad—
And I your daughter—do not water
         Down the significant
                  the truly magnificent
                           day I've had,
In just remembering—
         and dissembling
                  glad from sad.

No matter you're beyond the veil
And I am here and cannot see.
I know your love will never fail—
You're always watching over me.

And though I cry because I miss you—
Can not hug or even kiss you—
Still I celebrate within
         as I look back
                  recall the knack,
Of how you made me proud we're kin.

Dedicated to my Father   Jan
Ellis George Gray   June 2, 1992
on his 88th Birthday—
June 2, 1992
(died August 21, 1977)

GOD'S OTHER DIMENSION

I have a little silent friend.
Together daily—hours we spend,
And without words we comprehend—
The love we share—and we transcend—
Invisible barrier—that to some—
Might be a wall not overcome.

We use out eyes;—communicate.
In deepest sense we captivate,
Each other's souls,—anticipate—
Responses that illuminate,
The miracle that came as gift.
We do not even have to sift—
Or ponder how it came to be.
It's from our Lord;—for him—for me.

My silent friend—companion dear—,
Shares life with me;—another sphere.
We have the joy to co-exist—
He's faithful listener;—psychiatrist!
Not everyone can understand.
Just those who know such wonderland—
Of creature—human interchange.
And then such love they'll not find strange.

Dedicated to   Jan
Rochester Harry Whittier Kolb   September 20, 1991

What was true and expressed in this poem still remains true to this very day. Though the poem was written sixteen years ago, it speaks of the present and our precious relationship that ever exists and is eternal.

AN UNSEEN GUEST

There was a wedding that took place
But in the crowd 'twas not his face
That I could find.
And though I saw it in my mind—
I wanted him—
It was no whim!
For he had held her as a baby
And was there—'twas never maybe—
As she grew.
And she knew
This fine man's ways
For all her younger days
'Til she was eight.
And then the very heavy weight
Of his death was suddenly there;—
A young child's deep despair.

I know he stood 'neath woodland trees—
And that the soft and gentle breeze
Was his spirit there unseen—
At her wedding—in the green.

Dedicated to   Jan
Ellis George Gray
August 21, 1994—
the 17th anniversary
of his entering Heaven—
and the day after his
youngest granddaughter's wedding

HEALER

Often when I am sad,
   concerned or ill—
He'll clasp both paws around my hands
   with a will
To make me right.
And soon will come light.

He'll never leave my lap—
   nor ever nap.
Long hours shall pass
   he'll hold me fast—
For he is there to heal—
   and it is precious and surreal.

He is God's Angel, in disguise—
   —a joy forever—my divine surprise.

For Rochester   Jan
with love and gratitude   August 28, 1996

TAKEN

In the living of my life
   my Rochester always took part —
O it was like a knife
   thrust into my heart —
     when he was taken.

I did not want to waken —
   not see his little face,
There in his place
   upon me in sleep.

I just weep—and weep and weep.

For dear Rochester   Jan

Angelic Host

He sits upon my lap—gazing into my eyes—
All love—and fully aware I know his disguise
Revealed to me compassionately through the years—
In tender moments—or when I've needed breath—or been in tears.
And so when his gaze shifts to beyond my shoulder
And his eyes widen to become rounder and golder
In recognition,—and he moves his stare slowly to the ceiling
Then climbs gently up my being in that direction—I should be kneeling!
For I am in the presence of Angels that have to me been shown—
Through his awe and reverence,—and made known
By one who is one—and welcomes others here from day to day.
I feel their silent presence come our way.
And in this small room I sit in splendor—dumbfounded—
For by Angels I am daily surrounded.

I do not yet have his eyes to see—.
I only know a feline Angel lives with me.

Dedicated to   Jan
Rochester—   November 4, 1995
and our Angels

PURRING PAPERWEIGHT

What could be more beautiful than this—
Dear cat contemplating in silent bliss.
Upon my desk in unmoving pose.
So pure of heart—free of life's woes.

Profiled in window—backdrop of trees—
Wafting through screen—the gentle breeze—
Entices closing eyes to slowly raise
Upon blue lake in meditating gaze.

He nobly sits—so utterly trusting.
Because I love him—I am adjusting.
For on my papers he has been alighting—
Until he moves—I cease that writing.

I take my pencil and waste paper scrap—
And pen this poem on my lap.
Sweet honorable companion—eternal friend.
In your faithful presence:—I choose to bend.

Dedicated to   Jan
Rochester   May 5, 1991

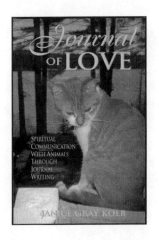

This picture was taken the day this poem was written. It later appeared as the cover picture of *Journal of Love.*

BLESSED BOND

One might think that with the passing of years
The level of enthusiasm might lower—
For this little creature who continually endears
Himself to me,—this gentle bestower
Of love and companionship and kindness—
Who sees only beauty in me—with blindness
To the ugliness of my faults and appearance—
Who plants his body on me—
And gives his constant presence as clearance—
Or stamp of approval—for all that I am and do,
And looks into my soul with large golden eyes that imbue
His utter love and faithfulness;—his assurance
That I am his and he is mine forever—,
A bond of strength and divine endurance.
If you think that passing years have diminished this joy,—
NO, NEVER!

Dedicated lovingly to   Jan
Rochester Harry Whittier Kolb   June 23, 1994
on the anniversary of our first meeting
and his adoption in
Rochester, New Hampshire
June 23, 1986

HAUNTING MEMORY

As I look back now and reflect—
    being much more circumspect,
I believe I can construe
    and understand what my Dad knew—
When we kissed and said goodbye—
    in hospital room that Saturday night.
And when I looked back with a sigh
    and saw he tried with all his might—
To raise one finger in farewell—
    it was because he could foretell,
We'd never meet;—no not embrace—
    nor ever again kiss face to face.
I did not know that as did he—
    and cannot rest that memory.

Written for
and dedicated to
my father
Ellis George Gray
on the 15th anniversary
of his death
August 21, 1977

Jan
August 21, 1992

GUARDIAN ANGEL

Little being filled with love—
You fit my heart just like a glove—
Revealing soul—in silent gaze—
And constant presence through the days.

Waiting in anticipation—
On bathrobed lap—your chosen station,
You remain—to underscore—
You long that I'll be strong once more.

Golden eyes in concentration
Search my eyes in adoration—
Little paws clasp firm my hand,
Telling me you understand.

Purring me to sleep and rest—
To make me well is your sweet quest.
Guardian Angel in soft fur—
White and marmalade comforter.

Dedicated to
Rochester Harry Whittier Kolb
(Chester)

Jan
April 20, 1991

JOURNEY TO GOD

What if I did not have you?
What if your passing away
was a form of annihilation?
O, no—instead it
was a creation—
a new form of life—
a way of spirit
and hope—
the realization
of an eternity
we would spend
together.
It was not an end—
but the beginning
of our soul's
journey
to God.

For dear   Jan
Rochester   July, 2006

MY SELLA*

The shadow of my soul—my heart
Is a soft and furry counterpart
Of all I am and feel and think—
And a most mysterious link
With God.—A consecrated connection
Sent by Him,—a perfection
Of love and joy,—one who is always there
Waiting to follow.—Such a pair
My Sella and I—for we
Are bonded spiritually—
One in Him—God drew no line.

My Sella, My Shadow—is divine—
And overshadows me in comprehending
The unseen realm. In gratitude for sending
This gift of playfulness, peace and protection—
I pause daily in awe and reflection
Upon this inseparable companion—this life force—
And I humbly thank Him—our Source.

Dedicated to   Jan
my Rochester—my Sella   April 10, 1996
with love
in the estimated
month of his birth

*Sella—means Shadow
  Taken from the poem by that name written by William Cullen Bryant

WITHIN

Your love grounds
    surrounds
        confounds.
You live within
    in silence
        where the din
            cannot reach.
It is there
    you teach
        and love abounds.

I whisper your name
    my heart is its frame
        and each letter
        is embroidered
            forever tightly.

I hear it within
where in a flame
of love
it burns
so brightly.

For   Jan
dear Rochester   October 31, 2003

THE VISION

My friend had a vision
That Rochester had risen
In a ring of Angels and Light—
He was lifted in love
To God above
On a tear-filled and dark Friday night.

My friend did not know
Of my sadness and woe
Or that Rochester was fading and ill—
He saw only release
And Rochester at peace
Apparently fulfilling God's will.

The vision of glory
That adds to his story
That is day by day ever on-going—
Gives peace to my heart
While we're briefly apart
And his presence on me he's bestowing.

For beloved   Jan
Rochester   June 2002
and in deep gratitude
to Chris Comins

UNVANQUISHABLE

Grief can not
　　　be forced to leave,
In loving deeply —
　　　deeply we grieve.
We live in sorrow
　　　and in anguish—
It's not an entity
　　　we can vanquish.

For dear Rochester　　　　　　Jan

CHESTER

Chester is a cat. He is very special. My grandmother loves him a lot. My grandmother takes him up to New Hampshire with her when she goes.

My grandfather makes scratching posts for Chester and Chester loves them. If you are sitting down, Chester will come up to you and sit on you and start to purr.

One time my grandmother had an ink pad out and was stamping letters. When my grandmother wasn't looking Chester walked through the ink pad and stepped all over the table. My grandmother didn't wash the paw prints off the table but she did wash the ink off Chester's paws.

Chester's real name is Rochester but my grandparents shortened it. My grandparents named him Rochester because they got Chester in Rochester.

Chester is orange and white. He is adorable. If you saw him, you would agree with me.

　　　　　　　　　　　　—Julia Rose Hudson

These endearing poetic thoughts about Rochester by my nine-year-old granddaughter written down for me are a gift of love each time I read them through the years. They express our love for Chester through her eyes. They express also our love for Julia in sharing them here. Julia just celebrated her twenty-fourth birthday and soon after made a visit to New Hampshire from Pennsylvania as she does frequently.

We are born for a higher destiny than that of earth. There is a realm where the rainbow never fades, where the stars will be spread before us like islands that slumber on the ocean, and where the beings that now pass over before us like shadows will stay in our presence forever.

—Edward George Buliver-Lytton

It is above that you and I shall go:
Along the Milky Way you and I shall go.
Along the flower trail you and I shall go.
Picking flowers on our way you and I shall go.

—Native American Song, Wintu

J anice Kolb, along with her husband Bob, are the parents of six grown children and have nineteen grandchildren. Their life has revolved around raising a loving family with religious values. In addition to raising their family, Janice developed a letter writing and audio tape ministry that gives encouragement and spiritual support to those who need it all over the United States.

Other inspirational works published by Janice Kolb include:
Higher Ground
Compassion for all Creatures
Journal of Love
The Enchantment of Writing
Beneath the Stars and Trees ... there is a place
Beside the Still Waters
Silent Violence
In Corridors of Eternal Time
Solace of Solitude
A Pilgrim on Life's Road
Cherishing
In a cooperative effort Janice wrote the book *Whispered Notes*,
with her husband Bob

Any correspondence to the author may be addressed to :
Janice Gray Kolb
P.O.Box 5
East Wakefield, NH 03830
jan@janicegraykolb.com

Visit her website at
www.janicegraykolb.com

Also by Janice Gray Kolb

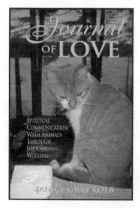

Journal of Love
Spiritual Communication with Animals
Through Journal Writing
ISBN: 978-1-57733-046-2, 180 pp., 30 illus., 6x9, $14.95

"Animal whisperer" Janice Kolb shares her heart-lifting journey of discovery as she learns to communicate with her beloved feline companion, Rochester—first by using her intuition and then by writing a journal of their "conversations."

"Once again the delightful and insightful Jan Kolb has provided all of us who truly love animals with another warm and wonderful book about how we may enter into deeper communication with our beloved pets. Journal of Love is destined to become a classic in the field of transpecies communication."

—Brad Steiger and Sherry Hansen Steiger, authors of *Animal Miracles*

Compassion for All Creatures
An Inspirational Guide for
Healing the Ostrich Syndrome
ISBN: 978-1-57733-008-0, 264 pp., 47 illus., 6x9, $12.95

A very personal book of experiences, confessions, and deep thoughts praising all God's creatures through photos, poems and meditations. This book lends an impassioned voice for examining animal rights from Mother Nature's point of view.

"Jan Kolb has written a very special book that will surprise you in many ways. Learning compassion and reverence by way of the animal kingdom makes perfect sense. She ponders deep questions and important issues which inspire her passion for all of life. Whether or not you join her crusade for the animal kingdom, you will end up thinking, and awareness leads to change."

—Terry Lynn Taylor, author of *Messengers of Light*

The Enchantment of Writing
Spiritual Healing and Delight
Through the Written Word
ISBN: 978-1-57733-073-8, 312 pp., 48 illus., 6x9, $17.95

Janice Kolb shares events from her life that illustrate how to train yourself to write daily. Her encouragement and guidance for writing lead naturally to self-discovery. By preserving your thoughts and experiences, you discover new sources of guidance and insight.

"There are angels cheering for us when we lift up our pens, because they know we want to do it. In this torrential moment we have decided to change the energy of the world. We are going to write down what we think. Right or wrong doesn't matter. We are standing up and saying who we are."

—Natalie Goldberg from *Wild Mind*

Higher Ground
ISBN: 978-1-57733-071-4, 176 pp., 16 illus., 5.75 x 8.75 hardcover, $14.95

Written freely, and from the heart, *Higher Ground* is a small treasure reserved for those who retreat into the silence and who wish to renew their purpose for living. It chronicles the experiences and thoughts of a woman on retreat in the woods of New Hampshire as she deals with personal fears and family problems and shares her faith.

From the book: *Like Thoreau—I went to the woods to be alone. Always this had been a dream—to stay by myself in our cottage in New Hampshire. Now that time had come. Depression and sadness had been settling in on me for too many months due to personal and family concerns. Each day's existence had become a hardship. My eyes filled with tears at unexpected moments. Though never intended, there were often times when I would sit for a minute to try to get myself together only to find later I had been there immobile for an extended period. Everything mattered intensely yet nothing mattered at all. The smallest chore was too big. Merely trying to begin anything was such an effort that I frequently just gave up completely....*

Beneath the Stars & Trees ... there is a place
A Woodland Retreat
ISBN: 978-1-57733-106-3, 372 pp., 47 illus., 6x9, $19.95

Beneath the Stars & Trees will help you withdraw from life's distractions and retreat to a place where you can see clearly the multitude of complex factors that make up your life. Share in thoughts and experiences which can open your mind to a world of peace and new possibilities for your life.

"Join Janice Kolb in a sometimes quirky, always perky, jaunt through lake-in-the-woods living, full of shapeshifting and kitty-cat angels, touching journal entries and frolicking poems, prayer chairs and little gnome tea parties—plus a spiritual encounter with a moose you're sure to remember forever."
—Michael Burnham, writer/journalist

"Jan's Woodland Retreat is a place teeming with animal and human life, and yet peaceful and serene. It is a perfect place to meditate, reflect, and renew your spirit. Beneath the stars and trees, there truly is a special place, and Jan's book will transport you there, as often as you wish."
—Mark Sardella, columnist, *The Wakefield Daily Item*

Beside the Still Waters
Creative Meditations from the Woods
ISBN: 978-1-57733-122-3, 276 pp., 11 illus., 6x9, $16.95

Beside the Still Waters is a personal view of prayer. Jan suggests a variety of ways to be in constant contact with God. These meditations can transform your prayer life into a source of personal fulfillment, power and strength. Many of these prayers may be familiar; others may be new to you. Being open to all that you read, you may discover new pathways to God and loving consolation. Though written from a Christian perspective, these prayers can be adapted to other traditions.

In Corridors of Eternal Time
A Passage Through Grief: A Journal

ISBN: 978-1-57733-135-3, 272 pp., 38 illus., 6x9, paperback, $16.95

As readers of Jan Kolb's previous books know, the author has had a deep relationship with her cat, Rochester. His sudden death plunged Jan's life into grief, and she began this book to honor Rochester and help herself and others experiencing grief.

The book is a passage through grief, written in journal form. It explores dreams, visions, walking, memory loss, depression, the consolation of cremation, examples of ways humans have grieved for humans, journal writing, ways to help ourselves, and through it all, the passage through mourning the physical absence of a beloved companion.

"Many of us are blessed by a deep love for animals. Jan Kolb is blessed by a talent for giving voice to this deep love. Through Jan, we connect to our deepest, loveliest feelings. Her gift is a natural gift, and we are truly the better for it." —Martin Scot Kosins, author, *Maya's First Rose*

Solace of Solitude
Afterlife Visits: A Journey

ISBN: 978-1-57733-153-7, 300 pp., 6x9, paper, $17.95

This book was begun to find consolation after the sad events of 9/11. Then the death of Jan's beloved companion, her cat Rochester, exposed her to a new view of life and death. Part 2 describes what she experienced and realized as a result. These realizations could not have come without solitude, which eventually brought solace. Perhaps by going aside in solitude you also will find solace in life and better understand the anatomy of grief.

"For all those suffering a loss of a dear spirit in their life—whether human or animal—this wonderful new book by Janice Gray Kolb will serve as a compassionate and understanding companion." —Brad Steiger & Sherry Hansen Steiger, authors of *Animal Miracles* and *Cat Miracles*

A Pilgrim on Life's Road
Guidance for the Traveller:
A Continuing Journey
ISBN: 978-1-57733-176-6, 184 pp., 6x9, paper, $15.95

A Pilgrim on Life's Road is the last of three by Jan Kolb to deal with grief—along with *In Corridors of Eternal Time* and *Solace of Solitude*. This book completes the author's travels to the place where questions and aberrant thoughts have been dealt with. This does not mean that there is an end to grief, but grief has achieved a new dimension and now contains elements of resolution. In resolving the many faces of grief we find that new avenues of experience develop new levels of understanding. The resolution of grief is not a single event, but a journey, which returns us not to what we were—for grief leaves an indelible mark—but to a place of sanity where growth can take place.

Cherishing
Poetry for Pilgrims: Journeying On
ISBN: 978-1-57733-205-3, 368 pp., 76 photos, 6x9, paper, $19.95

Cherishing contains some of the author's efforts at recording things that have made her who she is. Poem writing has become as much a part of her life as preparing a meal or taking care of her family. This is a book not only of poems, but comments about the source of inspiration. It's an insightful look into the author's experience that can cause you to think differently about your own life. Poems can make you laugh, cry, feel love, experience anger, and discover much about yourself. It's a different kind of a poetry book, and one you are sure to enjoy.

Poetry has been a very personal method of expression for the author since childhood. It is her hope that you will not only find pleasure in the reading and occasional rereading of her poetry, but perhaps find that poetry can become an avenue of expression in your own life.

from Blue Dolphin Publishing

A Guide to the Dolphin Divination Cards

One hundred and two oracular readings inspired by the Dolphins: A guide for the use and personal interpretation of the Dolphin Divination Cards

Nancy Clemens

ISBN: 1-57733-017-X, 384 pp., 6x9, paper, $18.00

Each reading is designed with a short preface for quick, easy reference, followed by a longer teaching and explanation. Woven through the readings are friendly counsel, a universal spiritual understanding, and an environmental message.

Dolphin Divination Cards

Nancy Clemens

ISBN: 0-931892-79-1, 108 circular cards, $13.00, boxed
Words of counsel and affirmation on round cards that fit comfortably in your hand

Wish for the World

A Daily Meditation for Personal & Planetary Peace
Keren Clark Posey with Ethan & Dyson Posey

ISBN: 1-57733-132-X, 384 pp., 5.5 x 6.25, paper, $15.95

A wish for each day of the year, covering such areas of concern as the environment, the earth's creatures, war, disease and famine. Each wish is accompanied by an inspirational quotation.

Summer with the Leprechauns

A True Story
Tanis Helliwell

ISBN: 1-57733-001-3, 208 pp.,, 5.5 x 8.5, paper, $13.00

During a summer in Ireland, Tanis was befriended by a Leprechaun. She recounts the fascinating relationship that developed and instructions on how humans can interact with elemental beings.

Orders: 1-800-643-0787 • **www.bluedolphinpublishing.com**